The G.I.F.T in Grief.

VOLUME I

Learning Lessons, Healing Hearts

Grief is both barren and blooming—
a landscape where loss and life coexist,
teaching us that healing does not erase,
it reveals.

— Dr. Paula Hollis

Published by Hollis House Publishing

www.paulahollis.com

ISBN: 978-1-969431-03-6

The GIFT in Grief

Foreword by Pastor Kevin Brown, The Perfecting Church

Grief has a way of finding us just when life feels most certain. It arrives uninvited, interrupting our plans, routines, and expectations. And yet, it often becomes the very ground where God meets us most profoundly. I learned this truth not in theory — but through tears.

Years ago, I lost my father — a man whose indomitable joy shaped my understanding of strength and faith. Not long after, I lost my pastor — the one who nurtured my calling and modeled what it meant to live fully surrendered to God. Those losses broke something open in me. I found myself wrestling with questions I couldn't answer and a conviction I couldn't ignore: that I had been living safe when God was calling me to live surrendered.

It was in the ache of absence that I began to hear a deeper call — a call to stop postponing obedience and step into the purpose God had written on my heart. Loss became the soil where new life began to grow. What felt like an ending became an unexpected beginning.

That's why this anthology, The GIFT in Grief, feels so sacred to me. It's not a manual for moving past sorrow — it's an invitation to walk through it. Each story in these pages bears witness to a holy paradox: that grief, while painful, is not wasted space. It is sacred ground. God still speaks in the silence of our mourning. He still comforts in the confusion of our tears. And if we let Him, He still transforms what was shattered into something that can shine.

When I officiated the homegoing service for Paula's beloved "Captain" – Martin – I saw this mystery of grief unfold again. His passing was sudden. His absence was deeply felt – not only in his family but throughout our church. Yet even in that valley, I witnessed the nearness of God: in Paula's quiet strength, in the embrace of a loving community, and in the steadfast hope that death never has the final word.

This first volume of The GIFT in Grief gathers twelve courageous voices who have dared to journey through loss and return with treasure. Their stories echo the eight GIFT themes that form the heartbeat of this work – Gratitude, Growth, Introspection, Intentionality, Focus, Forward-Thinking, Tenacity, and Transformation. These are not steps to "get over" grief, but sacred pathways through it – guiding lights for those who feel lost in the dark.

My prayer is that as you read, you'll sense God's presence meeting you right where you are – in your questions, in your pain, in your longing for meaning. May these pages remind you that your tears are seen, your story is still unfolding, and even here — in this fragile and holy space — something sacred is happening.

Grief does not erase our stories; it reframes them. And if we listen closely, we might just hear the whisper of grace reminding us: even in loss, there are gifts — unexpected, undeserved, and divinely prepared — waiting to be found.

Pastor Kevin Brown
The Perfecting Church
274 Delsea Drive
Sewell, NJ 08080
www.theperfectingchurch.org

DEDICATION

For every heart that has known loss
and still chooses to love again.

For the ones we carry in memory,
and the ones we carry forward.

For my Pastor, Kevin C. Brown, thank you for your prayers, support and opening this book with both a pastoral and practical perspective.

For Martin, my Captain — whose love taught me that legacy is not measured in years, but in how deeply we are known and remembered.

And for each contributing author who turned pain into purpose — Thank you! Your courage is yet another gift we give the world.

"Sometimes the most precious gifts are wrapped in the lessons we never asked for."
— Unknown

TABLE OF CONTENTS

The Framework - The G.I.F.T. in Grief: Learning Lessons, Healing Hearts

Grief rarely feels like a gift. It arrives uninvited—wrapped not in ribbons but in ache. Yet over time, if we lean in gently, we begin to see what loss can reveal rather than only what it removes.

This collection invites you to explore eight expressions of grace that often unfold in the tender terrain of grief:

Gratitude reminds us that even in loss, love lingers. Every memory, every smile, every sacred moment becomes evidence that what was shared still matters. Gratitude helps us honor what remains while acknowledging what's gone.

Growth asks us to become more than our sorrow. It doesn't demand that we "move on," but that we grow through. Like roots finding new ground after the storm, we learn resilience, empathy, and strength we never knew we carried.

Intentionality turns mourning into meaning. It's the quiet choice to heal on purpose—to rebuild routines, revisit memories, and move forward with care. Intention is how we participate in our own healing.

Introspection invites us to listen inwardly—to notice what grief is teaching us about love, faith, and self. When we pause to understand the landscape of our loss, we uncover not only pain, but perspective.

Focus anchors us when emotions rise and memories flood. It helps us attend to what truly matters: honoring our loved ones, tending our hearts, and rebuilding one step at a time.

Forward-thinking doesn't erase the past; it integrates it. It's how we carry our loved ones with us into new seasons—allowing their legacy to inspire rather than imprison us.

Tenacity is the sacred courage to show up again —imperfectly, vulnerably, but still present. It's the grace to keep breathing when the world feels still.

Transformation is the quiet revelation that while grief changes us, it can also refine us. Healing doesn't mean forgetting; it means remembering differently—with less ache and more awe.

Together, these eight elements form the G.I.F.T. in Grief—a process of learning lessons and healing hearts.

Each story in this anthology offers a glimpse into how loss can evolve into legacy, pain into purpose, sorrow into song.

As you read, may you find yourself reflected in these pages—and may each voice remind you that even in the ache of absence, you are not alone, and your healing still has holy ground to cover.

This is the G.I.F.T. in Grief - Learning Lessons, Healing Hearts.

Meet the Author - Phaedra D. Robinson

Phaedra D. Robinson is a resilience advocate and organizational development expert. She is the founder of Phaedra Denise Coaching & Consulting, LLC—a company specializing in personal and professional development. The company is committed to helping individuals and organizations unlock their full potential through clarity, confidence, and intentional growth. The firm offers workshops, coaching, and online programs that blend faith-grounded wisdom with proven strategies. These services create real transformation from the inside out.

Phaedra is the visionary behind the Better Than Resilient® brand. She is also the creator of the C.L.I.M.B. framework. This signature model helps individuals move beyond mere survival and embrace purposeful living, even in the face of life's most challenging disruptions.

As an adjunct professor with the Community College of Philadelphia, Phaedra brings over 25 years of experience in corporate leadership, adult learning, and organizational psychology. She is known for her compassionate yet strategic approach to change. Her work is deeply informed by her personal journey. In 2017, just after giving birth to her second daughter, she was diagnosed with lupus. That experience marked the beginning of her own climb—one of loss, adaptation, faith, and ultimately, renewal. Now in her eighth year post-diagnosis, Phaedra uses her voice, story, and expertise to help others turn pain into purpose and become their strongest selves—Better Than Resilient®.

Connect with Phaedra online:

Instagram: @phaedra_denise

Instagram: @BetterThanResilient

LinkedIn: www.linkedin.com/in/phaedra-d-robinson-msod-a223b085

Email: info@phaedradenise.com

Anchor Word: Transformation

Paula's Prelude

Some people enter your life as proof that resurrection is real. Phaedra writes about grief as both teacher and midwife – ushering in a version of herself she never knew existed. Through her words, you can feel the weight of loss giving way to lift. She reminds us that transformation isn't about forgetting what broke us; it's about learning to fly with the cracks still showing.

Grief is not limited to the loss of a person — it is the loss of possibility, rhythm, and routine. Yet even in its ache, grief reminds us that we once loved deeply enough to feel.

C.L.I.M.B. through Transition

Anchor Word: Transformation

I wasn't new to motherhood; my oldest was just shy of five, and my first pregnancy had been smooth, almost effortless. I had bounced back with ease, returning to work, family, and life as usual, with minimal interruption. That's why, when we decided to grow our family, I felt confident. I didn't want my oldest to be an only child, and I knew I had more love to give.

In June 2017, I gave birth to my second daughter. But this time, something was different. In the weeks after delivery, I couldn't shake a lingering fatigue. And I'm not talking about the normal exhaustion that comes from sleepless newborn nights. This was deeper. My body felt drained in ways I couldn't explain, and strange aches crept into joints I'd never had issues with—my wrists, fingers, toes, and even my knees. I brushed it off at first. I had a baby to nurse, a family to care for, and a professional life I planned to get back to. But eventually, I had to admit I didn't feel like myself.

I scheduled an appointment just before returning from maternity leave, around August 2017, to make sure everything was okay. My OB was on her own maternity leave, so I saw an associate, who dismissed my symptoms as typical postpartum and recommended Zoloft, an antidepressant. I knew that wasn't the issue and declined, then saw my Primary Care Physician. After listening carefully and running blood tests, my PCP suggested an emergency rheumatologist appointment. Knowing it would be difficult for me to schedule, my doctor made the call on my behalf. The rheumatologist, once he heard my case, brought me in the next week, on his birthday, if I recall correctly.

As I sat across from this new doctor, a young man with bright eyes and a direct, challenge-ready attitude, I felt both calm and confused. He didn't mince words, which I appreciated. He said, "You have all the markers that point to Systemic Lupus Erythematosus." Before he even read the test results, he knew my situation just from talking with my PCP. My age, my race, the timing after childbirth, and my symptoms all supported what the lab work showed. In that moment, being the controlling problem solver that I was, time seemed to speed up, and I went straight into solution mode. "Ok, so tell me what it is and what do I do about it?" is how I responded. (Learn more about Lupus here: Help Us Solve The Cruel Mystery | Lupus Foundation of America)

Once this new doctor took the time to explain in detail the severity of what I was up against, the treatment plan possibilities, side effects, and all the possible outcomes, time slowed down drastically. The optimism I'd clung to just moments before gave way to disbelief. All I could think was, "How could this be happening now, just months after bringing a new life into the world?" It felt like life had pulled the rug out from under me. Almost immediately after my diagnosis, my health began to decline as my condition progressed to Lupus Nephritis, impacting my kidney function. Within a few weeks, my blood pressure skyrocketed, my body began to retain massive amounts of fluid, and I was admitted to the hospital for 8 days. During this time, I could no longer nurse my newborn due to the amount and types of medication I was put on. I was informed that most of these meds would be necessary for the rest of my life.

What was happening to my life? As pain overtook me, it turned to anger and hurt. I was angry that, despite doing everything "right," I still got blindsided. Angry that I couldn't power through this like I had every other obstacle in times past. Angry that God, whom I had leaned on my whole life, let this happen at what felt like the most inopportune time. My world slowed down. My goals paused. My joy got complicated. I was no longer just a mother, wife, or corporate climbing professional. I was now a patient. A chronic one.

Though I made every effort to hide my pain, grief began to set in. Not the kind of grief that brings casseroles and condolences. But the kind that crept in on those quiet nights in the hospital bed when the lights were out and the visitors were gone, or when I was back home but my family was asleep, and my mind wouldn't stop racing. I grieved my energy. I grieved my strength. I grieved over the hair I was losing in clumps. I grieved the feeling of waking up and feeling normal in my own skin.

But underneath all the confusion, the fatigue, and the disappointment, I began to understand something painful and profound. I wasn't just grieving a diagnosis. I was grieving the loss of who I thought I was supposed to be. The problem-solving perfectionist who always had everything under control and a master plan for everything else. I grieved the loss of control over the life I had designed.

When people talk about grief, they often tie it to death. But there's another kind of grief that's harder to name. The kind that comes when your life is still intact on the outside, but inside, everything has changed. That's the kind of grief I carried. Lupus didn't just affect my body. It impacted my sense of identity. I was used to being the go-to person, the one who could find answers, push through deadlines, show up for everyone, and manage a full plate. Suddenly, my body said "no," loudly and often.

Some mornings, I couldn't get out of bed without pain. Some days, I'd forget things mid-sentence or lose track of where I was going mid-stride because of brain fog. All the while, I was expected to keep moving, mothering, working, and smiling. But I was breaking in slow motion. I watched my goals fade into the distance. I had always pictured myself climbing the corporate ladder with strategy and strength, but instead, I found myself deferring opportunities and questioning if I still had the capacity to achieve my goals.

It wasn't just physical fatigue; it was emotional erosion. Because no one teaches you how to grieve the life you planned for. There was no script for saying goodbye to a version of yourself that no longer exists. No ceremony for the ambition you once carried with pride. People saw me smiling on the outside, not realizing I was praying through pain. They heard my encouragement and saw me pushing through, but didn't see the private battle it took just to show up. It's like the lines in that popular Mary Mary song titled God in Me: But what they don't know is when you get home and get behind closed doors, man, you hit the floor and what they don't see is you're on your knees..."

To help myself just be able to show up, I tucked my grief inside and wore resilience like a mask. Yet behind closed doors, the grief surfaced stronger: I cried over clothes I could no longer fit due to the roller coaster ride of drastic weight gain and weight loss, grieved the stranger I saw when I looked into the mirror, mourned as clumps of my hair fell into the sink as I brushed it, and lamented the goals I had set for myself that I didn't have an ounce of energy to fulfill. Each of these moments deepened the question: Was I still "me" if I wasn't achieving, performing, producing? Somewhere along the way, my grief turned into survival. I became good at managing my condition, learning what triggered flares, how to read my body, and how to function through fatigue. I adjusted my routines, habits, and expectations. I learned to advocate for myself in doctor's offices and to track symptoms.

But inside, I wasn't healed. I was just surviving. There's a difference between getting through the day and truly living again. And I hadn't made that shift yet. Every time I looked in the mirror, I saw a woman showing up simply because she had to. She wasn't weak but on many occasions, she was tired of pretending to be strong. I didn't know it at the time, but I was approaching the end of a chapter. My grief wasn't over, but the way I carried it was about to change. Year after year, I adjusted. I adapted. I did what so many women do. I figured out how to function with my pain while still showing up for everyone else. But in year 4, something shifted. It was subtle, but undeniable. A nudge. A whisper. A quiet stirring that maybe, just maybe, there was something that I should be doing beyond just managing this diagnosis. In year 5, the nudge got louder. I started feeling a holy discomfort, like I was being invited to rise slowly, gently, but with intention. By the time I was in year 6, I started praying more intentionally about it. I didn't ask for a miracle cure, but I did ask for clarity. What was God trying to teach me through this? What was I supposed to do with this pain? I wanted to believe it all meant something. That the struggle wasn't wasted. That maybe my story could serve someone else, even if I didn't have it all figured out yet.

Then came year 7—and something shifted from internal to external. I began shaping those nudges and prayers into something more meaningful. I journaled. I dreamed. I reflected on my years of survival, not just through this, but also through other heartaches and challenges, and began to pull out lessons, patterns, and truths. That's when I started creating what would later become my personal philosophy for healing and forward movement. A mindset. A framework. A model I now call C.L.I.M.B©

And going into year 8, I made a decision. I wasn't going to just survive anymore. I wasn't going to keep managing life from the sidelines of my potential. I was ready to live it.

That shift didn't happen all at once. As a matter of fact, it's still happening at this very moment as I sit at my desk in my office at 5 am, writing this story while everyone is still asleep, and the sun rises slowly, peeking through my drawn miniblinds. It's deeply spiritual. As I reflected on everything I had endured, I didn't immediately recognize the timeline. I had been so focused on making it through each day, each flare, each season, that I hadn't paused to connect the dots. However, as my youngest daughter approaches her 8th birthday, something recently clicked. Watching her transition from 7 to 8 years old, gaining independence, confidence, and even a hint of sass, I felt something shift within me, too. By the way, her personality is everything I wish I had as a child. She is full of life and parrot-like energy, which is the total opposite of my Owl-like energy. Stay connected with me to learn more about the behavior and personality energies we all carry.

It was as if a weight had been lifted. I could see that she didn't need me in the same way anymore. She was growing, and so was I. In that quiet moment of reflection, I had a revelation: Her transition from 7 to 8 was and is mirroring my own. That's when I remembered the biblical significance of the number 7, which represents completion, rest, and divine fulfillment. As I prayed about the number 7 and what I was supposed to do with that information, it was revealed to me that the number 8 represents new beginnings, resurrection, and renewal. Could it be that I had reached the end of one spiritual season, my seven years of survival, and was now stepping into my eighth year of becoming? What if God was saying, "Well done. Now, let's begin again." The idea didn't just comfort me, it empowered me.

I wasn't starting from scratch. I was starting from experience. From faith. From strength that had been tested and refined. That's when the pieces of my personal philosophy began to fall into place. I examined the lessons, the shifts, and the transformation, and I built a framework that I could live by. One that I could one day share with others who also felt stuck between surviving and truly living. I call it C.L.I.M.B.©, and it began as my survival strategy but has become so much more.

- C – Confront the Challenge
- L – Learn the Terrain
- I – Imagine What's Possible
- M – Mindset Over Everything
- B – Believe in the Breakthrough

This model wasn't something I read in a book. It was something I lived repeatedly through challenging times and didn't even know it. And going into Year 8, I finally decided to take it on.

I used to think resilience was the goal. To bounce back. To hold it together. To survive. But now I know, resilience is only the beginning. Because if all we ever do is bounce back, we risk settling for who we were before the storm.

And I now believe some storms come to shift us, not just to test us. That's what lupus did for me.

It stripped away the version of me who believed success meant doing it all, all the time, without asking for help. It confronted the parts of me that measured worth by productivity and performance. And in the end, it introduced me to a version of myself I would've never met without the grief.

.... it introduced me to a version of myself I would've never met without the grief.

Yes, I lost things. My health was compromised, my sense of certainty in where I was going and what I was doing, and the control that I thought I had over various parts of my life, personally and professionally. But I gained clarity. I gained compassion. I gained an unshakable belief that I don't have to go back to who I was. I get to become someone better. That's the heart of what I now call being Better Than Resilient.

It means:

- You honor your grief without living in it.
- You make peace with what was, while building what's next.
- You stop chasing the old version of you and start embracing the becoming.

The C.L.I.M.B© framework gave me a language for that becoming. But what gave it life... was surrender. I had to surrender the idea that strength meant perfection. And accept that true strength is found in the rebuilding. More specifically, building back better. If you've read this far, maybe you're carrying something too. Not a diagnosis, maybe. But a loss. The loss of a dream. The loss of control. The loss of who you thought you were supposed to be by now.

If that's you, I just want to say this: you're not alone. And you don't have to be stuck. This might feel like the end of a chapter, but it could be the beginning of your eighth day. Your moment to rise. Not because it's easy, but because you're ready. You don't have to simply bounce back. You have permission to build back better. To C.L.I.M.B© to be Better Than Resilient. And when you do, you won't just survive your grief. You'll become someone your past self would be proud of.

Your pain is real and so is your purpose. If you're still breathing, you are still becoming who you are intended to be. So, here is my challenge to you: Don't rush past the pain. Pray about it and ask for guidance and the strength to endure. But also sit with it, study it, and let it speak to you. Instead of asking, "Why did this happen to me?" ask, "What can this pain produce in me"? Because every loss is a lesson, and within every lesson is a seed of something greater for you, and to be shared with others who are going through what you survived. But you must be willing to grow through it.

Meet the Author - Sheila D. Stewart

Sheila D. Stewart, affectionately known as MommaShe, is a devoted mother, grandmother, and mentor whose strength was refined through profound loss and unshakeable faith. Having endured what she calls her "double grief," she continues to share her story to inspire resilience, hope, and healing in others. Sheila believes that love never ends—it simply takes a new form.

Connect with Sheila via email at sheilad501@comcast.net.

Anchor Word: Transformation

Paula's Prelude

There is a rare beauty in a story that holds both heartbreak and resurrection. Sheila's journey reflects what it means to be twice broken yet still choose to bloom. Her faith became the bridge between loss and life, proving that transformation is not about forgetting what was lost, but about allowing love to take root again in new soil.

Twice Broken, Still Blooming

Anchor Word: Transformation

My name is Sheila D. Stewart, and this is my 'double grief' story. My journey began in the winter of 1972. I was an honors student and high school senior when I found out I was pregnant. I felt a mix of happiness, sadness, confidence, and uncertainty all at once. These emotions brought real challenges. Graduating was non-negotiable, so I focused on handling my pregnancy. I was young, yet faced grown-up choices. Determined to be responsible and careful, my family's faith and prayer quickly showed me what mattered most.

My high school sweetheart, Bruce Tunstall, and I sat down with my parents and shared "our" pregnancy. I knew I had to be prepared and have a clear plan in mind, since it was my responsibility. We told my parents that we wanted to do what was considered right at the time, get married and become a "legitimate" family, while I planned to complete high school. Those were the two definite decisions.

My parents listened and appreciated our thoughtful plan. They allowed me to get married and arranged for me to graduate from the school. Since I already had the credits, graduating was straightforward. Attending school in person wasn't possible, so I took my final exam at home, which I passed, earning my diploma. Organizing the wedding took priority; I planned to consider the graduation ceremony after my baby was born.

My parents and my Auntie Godmom, who made my dress, were more excited than I expected. They organized a small wedding and reception for us on January 27, 1973, and we got married at my parents' home. Even though some people were against it, prayer, planning, and determination helped us move forward as parents. As I prepared for this new chapter, I still heard doubts and gossip from others. Inside, I wrestled with self-doubt and hope, wondering if I was truly ready and if our young love could withstand what was to come. These thoughts were hard to shake and made me feel judged, which only increased my fears. Still, I held on to my faith and to

Bruce, trusting that our commitment would help us through.

On May 8, after 36 hours of labor, Tawana Nichole Tunstall was born. She brought joy and strength to our family, and we felt excited and humbled to be her parents. The doctors said she was healthy, but kept her in the hospital for three days of tests. Why, I wondered? What were they hiding? I kept asking questions but got no answers. I felt hopeless leaving the hospital without her. Despite the doctor's orders, I visited every day to check on my baby. Finally, on May 12, the day before my first Mother's Day, we brought Tawana home to begin our new life.

Settling into parenthood was challenging but rewarding. Both of my parents supported us. I clearly recall a quiet afternoon when my mom showed me how to change Tawana's diaper. Her steady hands guided me, and I felt grateful for her wisdom. My dad taught Bruce the importance of providing for family. While I had some childcare experience, learning from my parents was unmatched. I am forever grateful for their support, especially when I felt overwhelmed. Tawana brought us joy, highlighting the balance between new responsibility and youth. Sometimes I felt both capable and unprepared, learning daily how to manage, rest, and handle chores thanks to my mother's patience.

Life was starting to feel normal again, but the night of June 19 into the early hours of June 20, 1973, was anything but normal. My baby, who usually slept well, was restless and didn't want me to put her down. The room was quiet except for the ticking clock, which made the night feel even longer. I held her until 3:00 a.m. when she finally fell asleep. I rested as long as I could, drifting off around 5:00 a.m., but then my husband woke me up to say something was wrong with our baby. I never imagined we would find our baby girl in her crib, not breathing.

We rushed to the ER with my lifeless baby in my arms, trying to wake her with tears. I kept whispering, 'Please wake up, my sweet girl.' I had no answers and felt helpless. In the hospital, I felt like I was in a chokehold, thinking, 'This can't be real. What did I do wrong?' An hour later, doctors led us to a small room and told us our daughter was gone. My world collapsed. I asked them, 'Why didn't you save my child? What did you do?' It was indescribable. After giving birth at seventeen, just after turning eighteen, I lost her. I didn't think I could go on. Planning a funeral for a six-week-old didn't seem real; I prayed to wake up from this nightmare. How would I get through? After her funeral on June 23, I visited the gravesite daily, seeking clarity. I was an emotional wreck, feeling like a ticking time bomb.

I knew I had much to do, but I didn't know how to proceed. Despite careful planning, nothing went as planned. Comments meant to be supportive actually hurt deeply.

> "*You're young, baby*," someone said, a remark that felt like a dismissive wave, not acknowledging my anguish.

"*You were too young to have a child,*" another voice echoed, piercing through with the sting of judgment and blame.

"*You will have another,*" as if my precious daughter was just a replaceable part of my life, not the irreplaceable piece of my heart that she was.

All of these comments, and many others, felt like small cuts that made my grief even deeper. The sadness seemed endless, and the pain wouldn't go away. My smile faded as I tried to look strong, even though I felt broken inside. I want other grieving mothers to know it's okay to feel this way, and even though the journey is long and hard, hope can return with time. With help from my husband and parents, I tried to put myself back together and find some sense of normal life. I kept smiling through the pain, hoping these struggles would one day make me stronger and wiser.

...I tried to look strong,
even though I felt broken inside.

Two years later, in 1975, I was pregnant again, due on September 30th. I was still scared and carried many emotional scars, but I managed to hold my head high and face this pregnancy with grace and confidence. Even though people kept making comments, I chose to keep working so I wouldn't focus on their negativity. I didn't want any of that to affect my child. On October 2, 1975, my daughter Amber Shan'elle Tunstall was born healthy and happy. I held her close every day, determined to keep her safe from anything harmful. On her first night home, I watched her sleep, feeling a strong sense of responsibility. The room was quiet except for her gentle breathing, and I made sure nothing disturbed her. I felt trusted with the job of raising and protecting her. I decided that only my husband, my parents, and a few close family members could watch her when I wasn't there. I didn't trust anyone else to care for her, and I kept my guard up.

But just forty days after Amber was born, my life changed again, and the pain I already felt grew even deeper. On Monday, November 10, 1975, I received a call from St. Joseph's Hospital in Pennsylvania, instructing me to come immediately. My heart raced, and I felt like my world was about to fall apart again. My sister drove me to the hospital, where the staff told me I needed to identify someone. I didn't know who it could be. When I was taken to a patient's room, I saw it was my husband, who had died from a heart attack. Seeing him there, I felt weak and overwhelmed. I couldn't think or speak, and I just collapsed onto the bed, crying uncontrollably. I had now lost the only man in my life besides my dad. It didn't feel real.

Was this another nightmare? Why was this happening to me? I started to wonder if I was being punished or if I was a bad person who didn't deserve peace. Searching for answers and not finding any was hard, and making up my own only made things worse. I realized these thoughts were hurting me. I felt no peace or joy, and I didn't know why. My faith, which usually comforted me, felt far away. I questioned everything I believed and wondered if my prayers were heard. Even with all the anger and confusion, I tried to hold on to hope that my faith could help me through. Now, I had lost another loved one and was left with a six-week-old baby and even more anger than before.

Two years and five months later, I was planning another funeral, facing even more grief and resistance. I had to say goodbye again after another loss, and I was still not yet twenty-one. I wondered how I could keep going and rebuild my life. I relied on prayer, courage, grace, and the love and support of my parents. I knew I had a choice: give up or keep fighting to raise my daughter, who was a precious gift and deserved the best life I could give her. Was it easy? Not at all. It was painful, humiliating, and sometimes embarrassing. There were moments when I felt weak, but I kept going. I tried to turn every negative comment into something positive so I could focus on what really mattered. Now, I was visiting two gravesites instead of one.

I became a stay-at-home mom because I couldn't handle facing the outside world. I lived in constant fear, and the only way I knew to cope was to stay home with my daughter and my parents. I told myself I was fine not going out or doing certain things. But I realized I was letting fear and distrust of people and life take over. I knew I had to get control of it before it affected my mind, because I needed to care for and protect my child. When I considered returning to work, I knew I could only trust my parents to care for my daughter. I couldn't trust anyone else. In March 1978, after almost three years at home, I started working at Gloucester County College as an Administrative Assistant in the Financial Aid Department. That same month, I bought a two-bedroom condo for us. I was starting to live a little more, but I was still worried. I kept thinking, what if something goes wrong with my child? What if she gets hurt or lost? The worries seemed endless. Some people said Amber would grow up too sheltered because her grandparents were caring for her, but I knew she was learning good values, manners, and respect, just like I did. Most importantly, she knew she was loved and protected by her family.

These experiences taught me more than I expected at such a young age, but I am grateful for them because they showed me how quickly life can change and how important it is to appreciate everything. I had to grow up fast, but I realized I wasn't a victim. I was someone who had to adapt quickly, and I survived because I chose to learn from every decision I made. Getting married and having a child at a young age taught me to focus on life and make the most of each day. I learned to be strong and to keep a positive outlook, trusting that my faith in God would guide me. I also learned it's okay to feel all kinds of emotions, but it's not okay to blame others for how I feel. My actions and feelings are my own responsibility. To mothers currently grieving, my advice is to lean on those you trust, allow yourself to feel whatever emotions arise, and remember that your journey is unique and personal. Seek comfort in the support of loved ones and give yourself grace as you navigate through your pain.

I know I am a survivor. My faith, prayers, and personal relationships helped me get through all the pain and challenges. Looking back to when my journey began in 1972, I see how strength and faith have always been with me. Now, at seventy, my faith is still strong, and I have a close, loving relationship with my daughter, who is now married. We have become friends and respect each other's boundaries. I am also a Godmother and a mother figure to many, and I will continue to love and support them, because love never ends. I will continue to smile and strive to make a positive difference in the lives of everyone I meet.

She mothers from memory and ministers through her presence. Some women are chosen to nurture not just children, but callings, communities, and courage.

Meet the Author - Montgomery Hollis

My name is Montgomery Dreyton Hollis. Originally from New Jersey, I am also a proud Hoosier, earning my Bachelor's degree from Indiana University. I currently call the Virginia portion of the DMV home. I have a feverous passion for sports, music, and visual storytelling. I am a proud traveler, although my fear of new food and art museums keep me from exploring as much as I should. In my personal day to day, I can be found listening to various musical artists, laughing with friends, and working on building my community. Professionally, I work in corporate finance in the hospitality industry.

While I indulge in various hobbies and interests, my family remains my most treasured item. The loss of my father has had a significant impact on my life, and its impact is one I am still discovering. As I uncover my feelings and open up about my journey, I hope my words can inspire others, provide an important perspective as a young male, and show that true strength comes from vulnerability.

Contact Info:
Montgomery Hollis
mdhollis712@gmail.com

I can be found on Facebook as Montgomery Hollis, or Montee.Hollis on Instagram.

Anchor Word: Introspection

Paula's Prelude

Montgomery, aka "The Bridge", writes with candor about navigating early-career disappointments and the ache of pursuing purpose without the father who inspired his dreams. Through his reflections, he reframes failure, discovering that grief isn't only about loss—it's about learning to keep writing the script when life edits the plot.

Grief has generational weight — yet when one son stands to speak, he lightens the load for those who will follow.

For the Plot

Anchor Word: Introspection

Grief is not linear. It is nuanced, complicated, and a large web of feelings that can unravel at any instant. The pain you feel in one moment can be amplified by grief and pain that has laid dormant. Nearly 50 months ago, my father passed away. I was finishing Thanksgiving break during the 1st semester of my senior year at Indiana University. My brain was everywhere. The choice of where I would work full-time was emerging, my role as the bridge of the family became significantly more important, and most pressing was now the physical removal of my childhood hero. I stayed resilient, returned to campus to graduate from college, and began working for a Fortune 500 company a few states away from home after graduation. The full-time job I chose was a financial decision, not a personal or long-term professional choice. I know my father would have been proud that I was working in corporate America, but the dreams I expressed over countless dinners with him were still just unaccomplished goals. Throughout the ensuing months, each professional accomplishment was marred by a cloud of unfulfillment. The struggle between outward success and inward fulfillment became the root of my journey through grief. It furthered my grief, and the pressure to achieve those dreams I shared with my father began to be overwhelming.

As I journey through the pivotal years of my young adult life, I remain without a physical father figure to ask questions to, gain wisdom from, and use as a sideboard. Friends, family, and the seemingly omnipresent voices on social media attempt to fill the void. The suggestions from those present online are equally enraging as they are eclectic. Within my generation, particularly, there is a new phenomenon of doing things "for the plot." For those not up to date with the ever-growing list of Gen Z slang, this phrase is leveraged when an individual is unsure of doing something, but recognizes it may bring intrigue to the plot of their life. That random night you stay out until 3 in the morning? That vacation you take to Europe? The various dates you go on searching for the *one*? All these choices present themselves as events that keep our episodic life interesting. It is a great phrase to use in humorous practice, but lately, I have found myself studying its profundity. Often in life, we question why things happen to us. Imposter syndrome creates questions about positive experiences, and an overwhelming amount of questioning is related to the negative experiences we endure.

I recently went through a round of interviews for a potential dream job. The process was a laborious one, both mentally and in terms of patience. Over the course of a month, I completed an Excel test, had a Zoom interview, and participated in eight additional in-person interviews to demonstrate my competency as a candidate. As I finished my last interview, I was filled with confidence and a sense of purpose. After years of studying my field of interest, networking, and positioning myself in the right place, it finally felt as though the hard work had paid off. The position would be mine, and I felt I was on my way to making my father proud and fulfilling my promise. I booked a vacation to the beach and was told that I would receive news of the outcome shortly before leaving. A much-needed vacation appeared to become a celebratory event.

As fate would have it, the position at the moment was not mine. Many of my friends were aware of my journey with this role I had applied for, as countless prayers and group affirmations were made over those few weeks. Upon hearing the news, I was distraught for myself, but also embarrassed to share the outcome with others. With each update to those in my circle, the grief from the missed opportunity enlarged. During one of my conversations with a close friend, he shared that he had recently been laid off from his job. His radiant optimism despite the situation surprised me, and he shared that he felt blessed to have the job in the first place. Initially, the company chose someone else over him, and months later, reached out and asked if he was still interested in the role. It was a lesson in perseverance and faith. As we wrapped up the evening, we both reflected on our collective grief. My friend also experienced the loss of his father in college, and we expressed how failures in life loom larger without a father figure to guide us. The embarrassment I felt for failing my friends was a drop in the ocean compared to the disappointment I felt in not achieving my potential and honoring my father. I realized the real struggle wasn't just job rejection, but the challenge of living up to my own and my father's expectations after his passing. My mind can picture my father saying the idea of me disappointing him is irrational, and that he loves me regardless of my job title, but my ears still covet to hear that comfort directly from him.

The conversation with my friend did succeed in lifting my spirits for a moment. More importantly, though, it reminded me that my story is not over. My show is not cancelled. This moment of defeat does not have to be the season's finale. In the introspective moments that followed, a newfound perspective was formed, and I recognized that our lives are collections of stories meant to serve as testimonies and examples for others. I am not alone in my grief, and staying silent about my emotions may make it harder for someone else to express their own. In the past, my grief has sheltered me. Uncertainty scared me, and the idea of taking risks was unnerving.

...it reminded me that my story is not over. My show is not cancelled.

Now, I am working to accept the inevitability of failure and trust that the support of the community around me will sustain me. Grief is often detailed by the absence it creates in our lives. Yet it is more than the absence - it's a lens shaping what matters most and how I define achievement. I am currently learning to expand my perspective. Grief is complex, subtle, and encapsulates the human experience. For better or worse, grief forces you to examine what matters most in life; It is a gift of inevitable introspection and transformation. While landing my "dream job" would bring tremendous joy in the moment, the most important achievement or role I can have is loving those around me.

Meet the Author - Veniesha Vincent

My name is Veniesha Vincent. I am a Morgan State University Alumna with a degree in Biology.

I am a member of Delta Sigma Theta Sorority, Inc. and I reside in Philadelphia, PA. I have a profound love for random acts of kindness and helping others in any way possible. My current professional journey includes working as a medical assistant and biomedical researcher. Building on these experiences, I plan to pursue my medical degree in the near future.

Motivated by the everlasting support and encouragement of my Godfather, Martin Hollis, the strength and resilience of my Godmother, Paula Hollis, and the trust in God, I hope my story will resonate in the hearts of those who need it most, helping them find their way to peace through the pain, laughter through the tears, and joy in the time of sorrow.

Contact Info:

Email: Veniesha.Writes15@gmail.com

I can be found on Facebook as Veniesha Vincent, or Instagram and Twitter: @Venieshaaa

Anchor Word: Gratitude

Paula's Prelude

Some loves arrive by blood; others arrive by assignment. Veniesha's borrowed father became a lifelong blessing—proof that encouragement doesn't end at goodbye, it changes form. Where science names transformation, her spirit names gratitude: the steady choice to trace God in the details and let remembered love keep speaking forward.

Fatherhood is more than blood — it is the steady presence that shapes legacy, language, and love.

The Father I Borrowed: Encouragement Beyond Goodbye

Anchor Word: Gratitude

I've always been comfortable with death. Before I get too deep, let me introduce myself. I'm Veniesha Vincent, 28 years old, a biomedical researcher, medical assistant, and future physician. From a scientific view, death is the one thing we can count on in life. I've never been afraid to face or handle a dead body; understanding death and its finality has always come naturally to me. Spiritually, since I was a child, I've had a strong inner sense, a deep knowledge I couldn't ignore. I was never surprised by death because I could always feel when it was near. Not exactly who or when, but always a close loved one, always just days after the feeling. As I got older, this sense only grew stronger.

Some may call it premonitions, others may say it's discernment. I quite honestly don't know what to call it. If asked when I was younger, I'd probably say it was a curse. As I mature, I'm beginning to see the underlying gift in it all. Whichever word describes it best, I leave to the reader's discretion. However, by my own definition, it's simply 'when I know I just know'. Unfortunately for me, I've yet to be wrong. Perhaps that contributes to how I handle death. My perspective on grief has always differed from that of most people. When it comes to grieving loved ones, I've never been one to express my emotions through tears, screaming, or shouting. I wouldn't get angry or lash out; growing up in the church, I knew not to question God. I'd cope through writing or laughter, and memories of the good times shared. I would try my hardest to shift my perspective to believing their purpose on earth has been fulfilled. I took the reframe of "funeral" to "home going" seriously, telling myself that we were just borrowing them and God now needs them back.

All that went out the window when my Godfather passed. Unlike before, I had no unshakeable feelings, no deep, intuitive thoughts on what was to come, no motivation to shift my perspective, and not a care in the world about questioning God. I was completely blindsided, and suddenly, all the "composure" I thought I had when it came to grieving was obsolete. In fact, the first thing I did was question God. I had just spoken to my Godfather, Martin Hollis. Who I proudly refer to as my Uncle Martin. We talked about the plans God had for both of us. He was excited about what God was going to do next in his life, and I was equally excited to see it all unfold. If anyone knew my Godfather, they'd know he was a strong man of faith. An encourager to say the least. From that conversation and hearing how sure he was, I knew God wasn't finished with either one of us yet. They also say in church that "God makes no mistakes". Upon learning about my Uncle Martin, I thought that certainly God had made His first one.

Receiving the news changed everything for me. I'll never forget getting the call. I remember it as if it were yesterday. I can vividly picture the entire day and moment that my life changed forever. It was the Wednesday before Thanksgiving. I lived in Maryland and was at work at the time, debating whether to go back home for the holiday.

On a whim, my coworker wrote down either "stay" or "go home" on two small pieces of paper. She mixed the two together in her hands and prompted me to pick one. I chose the hand with "Stay". My coworker, unsatisfied with the results of her own game, still encouraged me to go home. Something in me also told me to go home, so I did. During my drive, my mom called, saying she needed a favor and to come straight there. She knows I'm one to veer off the path at times before getting to my final destination. I couldn't tell by her tone that anything was wrong, so I didn't give it much thought, but remained obedient. When I got home, between the look on her face and the deep sigh, I knew instantly that she didn't need a favor at all. She led with, "Your Uncle Martin..."

I heard her, but it didn't feel real. I wanted her to explain, but at the same time, I wished she would stop. My mind couldn't accept what she was saying. None of it made sense; it felt like it couldn't be true. I found myself thinking, I just talked to him. How could he be gone so suddenly? A heart attack? Why, God? Why give someone hope for the future and then take it away before it comes to pass? Why Uncle Martin, one of the few men who was always there for me? My mind was full of questions for God.

When I focused again, I heard my mom say we'd be going to my Godparents' house soon to see my Godmom, her best friend, and my Godbrothers. The news was sinking in, so I agreed and went straight to my car. I needed to be alone. I needed this not to be real. Tears streamed down my face as I let out the loudest scream I've ever made, the kind that almost chokes you. I couldn't process what I'd just heard, and for a moment, it felt like I couldn't breathe. I had never reacted like this before, but I couldn't stop crying. No matter how hard I tried, for the first time in my life, I didn't know how to pull myself together.

The drive to my Godparents' house felt unbearable. It was too soon. I was about to walk into the house where he had just passed away, and it was also the home where I had lived during high school. That place was full of love, laughter, guidance, and memories of Uncle Martin. As we arrived and my tears soaked my shirt, my mom gently reminded me to find the composure she'd seen in me before. Even though I didn't feel able, I understood. My Godmom had lost her husband, my brothers had lost their father, and if I was falling apart, I could only imagine how they felt. I knew I should try to hold myself together. When I walked in, one of the first things my Godmom said was, "You were his daughter." In that moment, my heart broke. Deep down, I felt like I had lost my father. I told myself that was selfish and maybe even disrespectful since I still had my biological dad. But honestly, no man had ever been there for me like my Godfather. Trying to "get it together" had never been so hard.

My Godfather was a one-of-a-kind man. Similar to most people, I have no memory of meeting him. He's just always been there. He was my encourager. My intercessor. He advocated for me behind the scenes and in front. He took my dreams seriously, not just with words but with actions. He ensured my success and spearheaded my move with his family. He believed in me so much that I couldn't help but believe in myself. It takes a special kind of person to live out the role of Godparent while parents are present and able-bodied. He treated, taught, protected, and provided for me as if I were one of his own. Not once did I feel I wasn't part of the family. In his eyes, I truly was. As hard as he worked, he even found time for my back-to-school nights and parent-teacher conferences. My anatomy and physiology teacher always spoke highly of him after those nights. I have yet to meet anyone like him. Maybe that's why I struggled so much with his passing.

Leading up to his funeral, I felt so angry. I couldn't understand why this had to happen, and if I'm honest, I didn't want to understand it either. I wanted things to be undone. I would see USPS workers and randomly burst into tears. Completely stunned by what grief had done to me, I needed an outlet, so I went to what I knew best. I put my heart on paper and let God take the pen:

An ode to my Godfather: God Ordained

So much I could say yet my heart is left speechless

This was all God ordained anyway, so I'll allow him to speak this.

Would you mind, if I could, I'd like to set a scene for you. Paint a picture. Emphasize that when God ordains one thing, he's simultaneously stirring up something bigger.

1992 St. Luke. Chester Pennsylvania. Denise meets Paula. That was a part of God's master plan. A friendship that would go on to last 20 plus years now.

Can I tell you it was never about Denise & Paula, it was always about this man.

You see, with God, there are no coincidences. There's just purpose & divine connection.

So it should serve as no surprise, that in 1997 when I arrived, I still received a blessing.

Uncle Martin was my Godfather. & instantly you'd think "God-ordained", I understand. But bear with me while I string things together here. There was something quite different about this man.

It wasn't about his exterior or the way he moved. Not even about his work ethic, although that conversation could last all afternoon. It wasn't about the typical Godfather role, though he exceeded that. None will ever compare. Or the lively "oh wow's" I'd so often hear.

It was in the way he loved me for free... that I knew it could only be God. The way he fathered me with no blood connection. God said, "She needs to see loyalty, care, & consistency from a father. Show her me on earth Martin," & He did it with no question.

So immediately when I heard the news, I felt angry. How could you show me the love of a father and then come and take him? I had to ask for God to open my mind. I didn't want my own sight cuz I know I see water, but God can see the wine.

What he revealed to me was something much greater. He said, "Every life touched by Martin now has a blessing to sow to someone else later. My child, there is no loss when heaven is awaiting. You'll take your Godfather with you in every seed that he gave you.

Oh, how this was all a part of my plan. Martin was preparing for you, 1992 in that church on Tilghman. Now his job is done, and he is finally resting. Hear me when I say, "I've done this all with intention."

He may be gone on earth-side, but he'll always be present in each memory that crosses our mind. & with those memories and gifts instilled, I urge you to do what he would do & follow God's will.

Take no lessons for granted. With him in mind, enhance it. Whether it be to utilize your gift to encourage, or to get in tune with your purpose.

To strengthen your relationship with Jesus or to dedicate your life right now because he's worth it.

This is the result when God is in charge and when he ordains. Because Uncle Martin was God's faithful servant, not one life will ever be the same.

So with this I say thank you. Thank you God for letting me borrow your Angel. & Thank you, Uncle Martin for being mine. I will miss and love you until the very end of time. Until we meet again."

-Love your youngest (God) daughter

After reciting my spoken word at the funeral, it took some time, but eventually clarity came. I've learned that there is no such thing as composure when it comes to grief and that grief is not linear. It comes in waves, and it looks different for everyone. There's no right or wrong way to grieve and no specific amount of grief one is allowed to feel, despite the nature or title of the relationship. Whether you lost a friend who felt like a sibling, an aunt who felt like a mother, or a cousin who felt like a best friend. Love is love, loss is loss, and therefore grief is grief, no matter how you slice it. A wise woman once told me, "No loss is less than because it looks different, and there are no levels to love, which in turn means there are no levels to grief." Grief is simply love with no place to go. And how fortunate are we to have loved and lost, rather than not to have loved at all.

Four years later, and I still have my moments of "why Lord?" I still get sad at the thought of not getting those "I was just thinking about you" calls anymore. I finally got the courage to open his last voicemail to me, and it was of him telling me a joke one of the children on his mail route told him. A true testament of the kind of person he was. It made me smile. I recently went to my 10-year high school reunion. Approaching the event, I reminisced on the fact that this was all my Godfather's doing. Meeting my forever friend and having the experiences that I had in high school wouldn't have been possible without him. That thought itself made me cry. More often these days, through my moments of sadness, stillness, or even just reflection, I try to practice gratitude. I ended up thanking my old coworker in memory of Uncle Martin. Hindsight is always 20/20, and now I see how God used her to be the push I needed when I didn't know I needed it most.

Everything was always divinely connected. It's the moments and memories as such that help me see God in the details. At this stage, I am now able to fully shift my perspective. I've rewired my thoughts and have a newfound mindset. A redefined focus and a reshaped understanding. From my scientific point of view, just like the Law of Conservation of Energy in physics tells us, "energy can neither be created nor destroyed, but transformed from one form to another". This helped me to see that I didn't lose my source of encouragement; it just took a different form. It looks different now, it sounds different now, while still having the same quality and effect. From my spiritual point of view, just as the Bible tells us, "to be absent from the body is to be present with the Lord" 2 Corinthians 5:8. I have more peace with his passing because I know one day I'll see him again. I still hear my Goddad's voice of encouragement and wise insight telling me that if I believe it, I can achieve it, with hard work, dedication, and consistency. His last powerful piece of advice still plays on a loop in my brain, "Time waits for no one, kiddo". The irony of it all, which once made me sad, now holds me up in times where his tough love is missed yet still necessary. I have more smiles than tears now. It's funny how God works sometimes.

...I didn't lose my source of encouragement; it just took a different form.

Unbeknownst to my uncle Martin, or really anyone, is that even in death, God saw to it that my Godfather still left me with encouragement that will last me a lifetime. What gets by me the most, on my easy days and my hard ones, is one of his favorite songs by Johnathon McReynolds. Thanks to him, I pray my battles always end the way they should, and I will always make a conscious effort to let my bad days prove that God is good.

Meet the Author - Lorina Marshall-Blake

Rev. Dr. Lorina Marshall-Blake is the president of the Independence Blue Cross Foundation—a private, charitable foundation established in 2011—and the vice president of community affairs at Independence Blue Cross. In her role with the Foundation, she leads strategic, programmatic, and operational efforts that advance its mission to create sustainable solutions improving the health and wellness of the community. Under her leadership, the Foundation has become a collaborator, innovator, and recognized thought leader in addressing emerging health needs throughout southeastern Pennsylvania.

As vice president of community affairs, Marshall-Blake develops and manages key relationships that strengthen Independence's commitment to its social mission. She is active in more than 30 professional and civic organizations, including the Anti-Defamation League and the United Negro College Fund, and she serves as an associate minister at the Vine Memorial Baptist Church in Philadelphia. She currently serves on more than 25 nonprofit boards and committees.

Anchor Word: Gratitude

Paula's Prelude

In every anthology, there are stories that carry the gentle power of lived faith – stories that don't just tell of loss, but of legacy embodied. Dr. Lorina Marshall-Blake reminds us that grief and gratitude are not opposites; they are dance partners in the rhythm of remembrance. Through her reflections on sisterhood, service, and surrender, she shows how the ache of loss can still move in step with the melody of thanksgiving. Her words call us to a sacred truth: even when absence hurts, gratitude heals.

Sisterhood holds what words cannot — shared laughter, quiet understanding, and a bond that time cannot undo.

The Sister Act: Grace in the Rhythm of Grief

Anchor: Gratitude

My name is Reverend Dr. Lorina Marshall-Blake, though I am still not entirely comfortable with the title, as in my heart I still find it hard to believe, but God deemed it so. I am the President of the Independence Blue Cross Foundation and the Vice President of Community Affairs. I am also privileged to serve as an Associate Minister at the Vine Memorial Baptist Church.

If I could, I would trade in all of these titles to share one moment with Patricia Alberta Richardson Evans, my one and only baby sister, whom I still carry in my heart to this day.

Since childhood (though there was a six-year difference between us), Patti and I have always been opposites. For example, I would wear Mary Jane patent leather shoes with frilly socks, and Patti would wear suede moccasins. I must admit that even though we saw the world differently, we fiercely loved each other. And, there were times when she was the big sister, and I was the little sister.

However, throughout our relationship, there were times that we shared, even when we may have disagreed vehemently. Often, this was the case with my clothes. And fortunately, or unfortunately, we both shared breast cancer. It was in 1993 that I was diagnosed with breast cancer, but it was early and has resulted in my being a twenty-two-year breast cancer survivor (no chemo, just radiation) Thank you, Lord!

In 2015, Patti was diagnosed with breast cancer. Unfortunately, even with the knowledge of my breast cancer, this did not prompt her (I'm still mad at you, Patty (lovingly) to get tested. When she did it, she was further along than I had experienced. But not to worry, her big sister was in it to win it with her. Of course, I am the fixer (right). Thus, the journey began over five years ago, when we thought we had beaten this disease. And who would have thought after five years (which suggests you made it) that it would come back like a roaring lion and take her life. On March 23, 2019, as her family sat with her, sitting in vigil, hoping for a miracle, she quietly slipped away. But she did it her way. We did not see or hear her last breath. It was so, Patti. When we decided to leave her for the evening and go home for the night, she left this world as we knew it. Yes, when we left, SHE LEFT!! Yes, the songwriter was correct. Soon, she was done with the troubles of this world. She had gone "HOME" to Live with Her God! She was gone!

My Journey

Yes, Patti —my baby sister, my only sister —was gone. Although we don't understand the unknown, Scripture says in 2 Corinthians 5:8, "To be absent from the body is to be present with the Lord." I have to say and believe she is in a better place when I remember how she suffered. I would be remiss if I didn't say that I was grieving even before she passed away. One day, as I sat beside her, feeding her my homemade okra, tomatoes, and corn (that she loved), a tear rolled down her face, which I believe was a signal to both of us that it wouldn't be long. It brought back memories of the constant visits to chemo, the eventual removal of her left breast, the loss of hair, and the Lolita wigs. It also brought back my anger with her when she decided that enough was enough. She was done with chemo and everything that went with it. She wanted to go home. She didn't want to be in the hospital. She, no matter what, was relying on her F.A.I.T.H. Fully and Intently Trusting God, no matter the outcome.

Meanwhile, I was bombarding heaven, praying and asking for a miracle! She was indeed a courageous warrior, taking on this cancer with everything she had.
I believe one of my favorite times/moments with Patti was when we would go together for her chemo treatments. We always took the frog that sits on my bed, even today. We shared the acronym for FROG - Fully Relying on God. But God, I was relying on you to keep her body. But you didn't. Even so, I had to remind myself that God is still good. Not just sometimes, when things are in our favor, but all the time. God is Good! A highlight for me was Patti's celebration of life. I believe over a thousand people came to say their personal goodbyes to

this phenomenal, caring, and loving woman who not only knew Jesus as her Lord and Savior but truly lived and breathed His word. I shall never forget, and I share here the poem Patti's daughter composed and dedicated to her mom, entitled "Dear Mommie."

Dear Mommie,
Selfless, kind, and loving...where do I start...
I feel like I just lost all circulation in my heart ....
My heart is beating, but I don't feel the beats...
I know I'm walking, but I can't find my feet...
Trying to clear my thoughts, but it's on repeat....
I've never endured a pain .... that cut so deep...
Thinking of you is easy; I'll do it each day, but there is an ache
within my heart that will never go away...
My life has changed forever, I will never be the same..
But if you look on the bright side, look what heaven gained..
Your spirit would uplift and light up a room...
I know I'm being selfish, but you left us too soon...
Tear puddles cloud my vision from sight...

It is so difficult trying to sleep at night...
Dance was your passion, it was one of the many things we shared...
Oh, how I'll miss your soft curly hair...
Your kisses, your warm touch... I'll miss you so much...
I'm thankful for you and how you made me the woman that I am....
Thanks for always believing in me and telling me I can...
This is the hardest thing I've ever had to do...
Who will hug me and hold me as tight as you...
You've touched oh so many lives...
You were so happy to help that it would make you cry...
No more pain, no more suffering, no stress...
Just endless peaceful nights in eternal bliss...
I'll keep your legacy alive,
Even though a piece of me has already died..
You are still my twin, my God knew you were too good to be in this world of sin...
You were a fighter even until the end...
Mommy, you will always be my best friend..
Thinking of you is easy, I'll do it each day....
But, there is an ache within my heart

That will never go away...Numb.

I love you, bubble, and I will make you proud.

Love,

Chloe Evans.

This ache in Chloe's heart is also an ache in my heart that will never go away.

Another moment during her homegoing that encouraged me was when a young woman performed a praise dance, singing, "I shall wear a crown." Patti was a praise dancer and her light always shined when she danced. It was as if she was dancing with the Lord with childlike abandonment. Just her and her Lord. Oh, what I would have given to be part of the dance! In my creative sanctified imagination (CSI), I could see her dancing in heaven to her favorite song, "My God is Good! Knowing, without a doubt, that he saved her soul and brought her out of darkness into the marvelous light. Yes, God Is Good!

Even now, my memories of the two of us growing up together flood my mind and are tucked away in a special corner in my heart. For three consecutive summers, Patti and I would visit my two aunts (my father's sisters) and my uncle in Clinton, North Caroline. For two weeks, we would experience Southern Hospitality together with our family. This was our time together, free from children, husbands, jobs, and other responsibilities. It was just me and her, commonly known as "the Sister Act." And during this time, from all appearances, Patti was doing well, even though she was still doing maintenance.

My Gift Word

"While grief may reflect what was lost, gratitude is how we continue to honor what was good..."

My gift word is gratitude. Even though being grateful didn't erase my grief, it enabled me to intentionally focus on what is good and meaningful in Patti's life that I hold dear. Patti was indeed a bright light, and although she has passed, her light still shines and will forever shine. Yes, losing her was and is still painful, but I am grateful that she was and is and will continue to be a part of who I am. Most of all, I am grateful for the times we shared, even during challenging times. Special moments when we explored the Word of God together. It has been said and suggested that 'gratitude can help one move from "Why did this happen to Patti?" to "I'm so thankful and grateful for what we shared when she was healthy and full of life, and even those moments when I held her hand to comfort both her and me." Oh, to be able to hold her hand again as we ministered to each other in those silent moments when she could no longer speak. In those moments, there was a rhythm in the silence when our spirits connected without a word even being spoken,

Now, I believe I better understand how grief and gratitude can coexist at the same time. It is yet a season in my walk, and daily I must determine how I desire to live. But more importantly, living genuinely with my grief, acknowledging and embracing it wholeheartedly, and creating space for gratitude. It means letting go of what I cannot change and reframing the perspective that I don't have to choose between grieving and gratitude. While grief may reflect what was lost, gratitude is how we continue to honor what was good while Patti was with us, even as we mourn her absence.

Some stories invite us to linger. They remind us that healing does not rush — it rests, re-centers, and reclaims what still has meaning.

Meet the Author - Rose Bailey Joseph

Rose is a “catalyst for destiny” dedicated to transforming lives and multiplying souls in the Kingdom of God. As a Destiny Coach and transformational leader, she carries the proud legacy of her parents while serving as a Licensed Elder and Intercessor at her church.

Rose is an Author, Maxwell Leadership Certified Coach, Speaker, and Trainer, with a Harvard Online Business School ‘Strategic Leadership’ certification. She is an Executive Senior Director with over 30 years of global experience leading and transforming organizations. She is currently completing her MBA in Digital Transformation and Organizational Change Management, with the goal of a Doctorate of Business Administration (DBA) in Strategic Leadership.

Rose launched her Leadership Academy in 2024 to create a supportive environment where leaders can receive training, network, develop leadership strategies, access resources, and receive in-the-moment coaching. The vision is to help leaders "lead to grow, and grow to lead."

Visit here website to learn more:
https://coachrosebaileyjoseph.com

Anchor Word: Tenacity

Paula's Prelude

Some tenacity clings tighter; Rose's tenacity surrenders. In her hands, strength is not forced—it's formed. Brick by brick, breath by breath, she shows us how God rebuilds what grief has unraveled, turning ruins into refuge and weakness into a quiet, enduring might.

Love is never forgotten, even when memories fade. Dementia may touch the mind, but it cannot erase the imprint of the heart.

Brick by Brick, Breath by Breath

Anchor word: Tenacity

It's interesting—you never really know where you are on your healing journey until you're asked to share it. Writing about it makes the experience even more vivid and undeniable. At brunch, I listened to a dear friend describe how sharing stories of grief can help others heal. In that moment, I felt called to confront the grief I'd hidden away and begin my own healing journey to help someone else along the way.

My name is Rose Bailey Joseph. I recently wrote a book titled God? We Need to Talk—a book about conversations with God through the stops, starts, detours, and divine interruptions on the journey to destiny and healing. Reflecting on my experiences, I'm grateful that many detours became divine redirections, guiding me back to where I was always meant to be. In my book, I briefly mentioned my mother's illness and passing in 2003–2004. This period, though it marked a 40-year milestone, became one of the most challenging times I faced. That loss, one of several major blows, shifted my life. While writing, I realized there was more to share about how that loss shaped me and my healing journey.

I began writing the chapter, but it was ultimately excluded from the final manuscript. Why? Because I had not yet completed the journey of healing. I just was not ready. My mother, Carmen Mae Bailey, died in March 2004, a week after Mothering Sunday. During that time, I also faced divorce, lost friendships, and financial strain, while pausing my ministry to rediscover myself. The umbilical cord may be physically cut, but its spiritual connection endures. For me, it felt violently severed, leaving me spiritually adrift—hence, God? We Need to Talk. Through pain and process, I learned about healing and God's sustaining power. Today, I share my story to testify to both loss and healing.

My prayer for you as you read is this: that you do not read out of curiosity about my journey and my fellow authors, but that you may also find healing. That you would cry the tears you've held back. That you would scream out loud when you need to, sit in silence when necessary, and allow your heart the full space to grieve. Finally, above all else, may you choose to rise. Rise fully. Rise completely. Rise divinely—into a place of healing, into a place of tenacity, prepared and strengthened for your next chapter. May your story, too, become a beacon of hope. I could share many stories, each part of grief and healing. As I mentioned in my book, losing my mother marked the most challenging season of my life.

In a chapter titled Queries and Conversations, I opened with Psalm 142:1–4, where the Psalmist David cries out in desperation:

> "*I cry out to the Lord with my voice;*
>
> *With my voice to the Lord, I make my supplication.*
>
> *I pour out my complaint before Him;*
>
> *I declare before Him my trouble...*"

That cry felt so personal. The Psalmist's lament echoed my own internal questions: Is God listening? Does He understand? Will He really come through for me? Had he actually given me more than I could bear? I had come to a breaking point. Everything I thought I understood, everything I had built, all that I had hoped for, was unraveling. And the unraveling wasn't gentle. It was shaking, sudden, and seemingly relentless. And yet, it felt necessary. The old had to fall apart, the rubble cleared, so the new could be built.

But I didn't go down without a fight. My resistance and struggle to hold things together started years before my mother's illness, beginning as early as 1998. For two years, I pretended nothing was wrong, desperately trying to hold back a flood with my bare hands. By 2000, those defenses gave way. From 2000 onward, I embarked on a four-year journey marked by confession, revelation, healing, and a gradual process of transformation. With each new phase, emotions surfaced, each wave taking away pieces I thought essential, until I could finally accept what God was doing to make me strong. This transformation—from crawling caterpillar to soaring butterfly—was gradual but necessary. So here I am, and here you are: not just a story of grief but of tenacity. It's the strength to walk even as your legs shake, to rebuild and stand strong, declaring, "The God I serve is mighty to save."

But here's the part I love: I didn't gain by tenacity and strength through striving. I gained my strength through surrender. Scripture teaches us that God's strength is made perfect in our weakness (2 Corinthians 12:9). I wasn't going to get through this season by pushing harder. I had to be emptied so God could fill me. I had to be brought low so He could lift me high. And that's when the deep work began. My mother's diagnosis of Alzheimer's came at a time when I was already emotionally fragile, having come to terms with the need to file for divorce. As a family, we had chalked up her forgetfulness and occasional confusion to age, fatigue, or stress. But then came the misplacements, the wandering, the blank stares, the missed names, and the realization that this was more than just the natural effects of aging.

I gained my strength through surrender.

Watching a loved one, especially your mother, slowly slip away is a living loss. You lose them before you lose them. It isn't just forgetting keys—it's names, faces, history, relationships. Alzheimer's steals connection and family stories, scrambles time, and erases context. Conversations become hollow, repetitive, or confusing. Caregivers grieve again and again, without closure. My family gave all we could, each in our own way. We watched the matriarch slip away while managing careers, children, and private struggles. There were tensions and unspoken questions: How are you coping? Do you need help? Are we doing enough? In truth, we were quietly drowning. For me, Alzheimer's gave me space to hide my unraveling. As my mother's mind faded, I shared secrets with her, knowing she might not remember. Sometimes she gave comfort or wisdom; other times, she stared past me. Regardless, I found comfort.

One day, I made a bold decision. I cut off all my hair. It was symbolic, a shedding of weight, an external reset to match the internal one I was craving. When I walked into her hospital room, unsure if she'd recognize me, she looked up. A moment of lucidity flashed across her face. She blinked, tilted her head slightly, and said, "Where's your hair?" I smiled, relieved. "I just needed a change, Mommy." She glanced down at the word search on her lap, picked up her pen, and said in that knowing, gentle voice: "Well, as far as I know, I only have two sons. So, make sure you grow it back." A laugh-out-loud and beautiful moment. That was my mother. Witty. Sharp. Honest. And though brief, that moment was oxygen to my soul. I laughed and cried on the drive home. But most days were not like that. Most days, I wept in my car, shouting at God, "Why would You take her like this? Why this way?"

March 28th came—the day my mother went home to the Lord, her wedding anniversary. I pictured her welcomed by my father, reunited on the day they once said "I do." I wasn't ready. I became the project manager, arranging, designing, purchasing, and coordinating. We gave her a beautiful celebration, honoring her and her reunion with Daddy. She could now rock Veronica, her baby who died young, and hug Martin, her firstborn, who left too soon. Back home, I collapsed on the lounge carpet. I wept uncontrollably and whispered, "God, I can't let this destroy me." Though I knew better, I began to "marshal" myself—not in God's strength, but my own. It helped me survive, but not heal. I kept my emotions in check, kept moving, kept smiling. I survived by compartmentalizing, as many of us do. Life moved on, and I was grateful for my new destiny. Within two years, I remarried, moved to a new country, and started a new chapter with an amazing man and family. But Mother's Day haunted me. I avoided church, ignored posts, sent flowers, but hid in my grief in the U.S. I told my husband Karl I was "fine," but by evening I was in tears. He didn't know what to say, and I didn't know what to ask for. In year six, during a friend's women's conference, I let the walls fall. I peeled back the curtain, allowed myself to feel, and opened the box I'd shut for years. Everything poured out. I fell to the floor, weeping like a child. My heart was racing so hard that I thought it might break. And then I heard Him:

> *"In your weakness, I am made strong. I never left you. I never forsook you. I will give you everything you need. You will run and not grow weary. You will walk and not faint. And I will give you your mother's mantle."*
>
> *"I will give you her wisdom. I will give you the stature I poured into her. And people will look upon you and call you blessed. You will become a mother in your community."*

Loss changes us. It strips us. It exposes the tender places we tried to cover. But if we allow it, if we surrender the rubble of what was, God will use that very brokenness to rebuild us stronger, taller, and more rooted in Him. The journey through grief is not a linear process. It doesn't respect calendars or milestones. But God walks with us through every wave, every silence, and every storm. What I've learned through the loss of my mother, through the long nights and hidden tears, is this: you don't have to be strong to be rebuilt. You just have to be willing to surrender. God does not despise your weakness. He meets you there. And from that place, He builds strength, not of the flesh, but of the spirit. A strength that holds others. A strength that shines through compassion. A strength that quietly declares, "I have been through the fire, but I do not smell of smoke." (Daniel 3:27)

So, if you are reading this and carrying your own grief—whether fresh or long buried—know this. God can and will rebuild you. But He does it best when you let go. "My grace is sufficient for you, for My strength is made perfect in weakness." - 2 Corinthians 12:9

TENACITY: 8 Steps to Healing from Grief

With Lessons from the Book of Nehemiah

T - Take Time to Feel

Grief demands attention. Don't rush through it. Take time to sit with your emotions, cry when needed, and acknowledge the depth of your loss.

"To everything there is a season... a time to weep, and a time to laugh; a time to mourn, and a time to dance."

— Ecclesiastes 3:1, 4

Nehemiah's Lesson:

Before building anything, Nehemiah sat down and wept over the brokenness of Jerusalem. He fasted and mourned before taking any action (Nehemiah 1:4).

Grief is sacred. Don't skip it.

- ➢ *Healing Step: Set aside intentional moments for prayer, journaling, and quiet reflection.*

E - Entrust the Pain to God

Grief is too heavy to carry alone. Release your sorrow into God's hands. He can handle your tears, your anger, your confusion.

"Cast your cares on the Lord and He will sustain you."

— Psalm 55:22

Nehemiah's Lesson:

Nehemiah consistently entrusted every obstacle and emotion to God in prayer. Whether facing opposition or carrying grief, he turned to God first (Nehemiah 2:4; 4:9).

Prayer was his foundation. Let it be yours.

- ➢ *Healing Step: In prayer, say aloud: "Lord, I give this pain to You. I can't carry it, but I trust You will."*

N – Nurture Your Soul

Grief drains you spiritually. Nourish your inner life with worship, scripture, and time in God's presence. Let Him fill your emptiness.

"He restores my soul..."

— Psalm 23:3

Nehemiah's Lesson:

Nehemiah called the people to return to the Word of God. After physical rebuilding, he prioritized spiritual renewal—reading scripture, worshiping, and restoring joy (Nehemiah 8).

Restoration begins from the inside out.

- ➢ *Healing Step: Read one comforting Psalm daily. Play worship music that ministers to your spirit.*

A - Accept the Journey

There is no perfect timeline for grief. Accept that your process may look different from others— and that's okay. Give yourself grace.

"My grace is sufficient for you..."

— 2 Corinthians 12:9

Nehemiah's Lesson:

The rebuilding of Jerusalem was a challenging endeavor. There were threats, delays, and discouragements—but Nehemiah stayed committed to the process. He adapted, but he didn't give up (Nehemiah 6).

Accept the journey, even when it doesn't go as planned.

- ➢ *Healing Step: Journal your grief journey without judgment. Acknowledge progress, even if it's slow.*

C - Connect with Others

Isolation fuels sorrow. Open up to trusted friends, family, a counselor, or your faith community. Healing often happens in relationship.

"Two are better than one... if either fall, one can help the other up."

— Ecclesiastes 4:9–10

Nehemiah's Lesson:

Nehemiah rallied the people to build together. Families worked side by side on the wall. They found strength in unity (Nehemiah 3).

Your healing is not a solo project. Invite others in.

- ➢ *Healing Step: Reach out to someone today. Let them walk with you.*

I - Invite God to Heal the Hidden

Grief often exposes wounds beneath the surface—old fears, regrets, or unresolved pain. Let God into the hidden places.

"Search me, O God, and know my heart..."

— Psalm 139:23–24

Nehemiah's Lesson:

Once the wall was rebuilt, Nehemiah addressed inner corruption, injustice, and compromise.

(Nehemiah 5 & 13). True healing required cleansing both the outer and the inner life.

Don't just rebuild—let God reform what's unseen.

- ➢ *Healing Step: Ask God in prayer, "What do You want to heal in me through this loss?"*

T - Turn the Pain into Purpose

God never wastes pain. As healing unfolds, allow your testimony to bring comfort to others.

Turn your tears into ministry.

"You intended to harm me, but God intended it for good..."

— Genesis 50:20

Nehemiah's Lesson:

Nehemiah's grief became a mission. What broke his heart became his God-given purpose. He didn't just mourn the ruins—he rebuilt them (Nehemiah 2:17-18).

Your pain can become someone else's permission to heal.

> ➢ *Healing Step: Write or speak one part of your story. Share it with someone who may be hurting.*

Y - Yield to the New

Grief changes us. Let it. Yield to the new version of yourself God is forming—a stronger, softer, wiser version, anchored in His love.

"Behold, I am doing a new thing..."

— Isaiah 43:19

Nehemiah's Lesson:

After rebuilding the city, the people made new covenants, new commitments, and embraced a new identity. The past was honored, but the future was embraced (Nehemiah 9–10).

Yielding to the new is how we honor the old.

- ➢ *Healing Step: Reflect: Who am I becoming through this? What new thing is God doing in me?*

Final Encouragement:

Just like Nehemiah, you may begin your journey in tears, but you will end it in testimony.

What once broke you will not define you. What once silenced you will empower you. What once left you feeling abandoned will become the very evidence of God's abiding presence.

Let God rebuild you—not just brick by brick, but breath by breath.

Meet the Author - Tikeena Sturdivant

Tikeena Sturdivant is an author, speaker, grief coach, and trauma advocate who transforms personal loss into purpose-driven healing. She is the founder of The Purpose Ark, dedicated to helping individuals navigate grief, trauma, and life transitions. Her journey was profoundly shaped by the passing of her daughter, Trinity Briana, to SIDS — an experience that became both the deepest heartbreak of her life and her reason to keep going.

Deeply passionate about working with youth, Tikeena is pursuing her master's degree in Community and Trauma Counseling at Thomas Jefferson University with a concentration in childhood trauma and play therapy. She is committed to equipping young people and families with the tools to heal, express themselves, and thrive beyond adversity.

Tikeena shares her story often, inspiring others with her message of resilience, faith, and the power of turning pain into purpose. A devoted mother to her daughter Serenity Sevyn, she continues to honor Trinity's legacy by creating spaces where others can find hope, healing, and the courage to bloom after loss.

Ways to connect with me:

Instagram: @thepurposeark

Email: thepurposeark@gmail.com

Anchor Word: Tenacity

Paula's Prelude

There are stories that hold their breath before you read them. Tikeena's is one of those. It is both lament and rebirth – the kind of testimony that reminds us that motherhood doesn't end at the grave. She writes with the strength of a warrior and the vulnerability of a mother who still hears heaven whisper her child's name. Through her honesty, she gives permission to every grieving mother to keep breathing, to keep becoming, and to find purpose inside the pain.

Life is not measured by duration but by donation. Even the briefest heartbeat can leave a lifelong imprint of love.

From Graveyard to Garden

Anchor Word: Tenacity

The morning I found my daughter lifeless will never leave me. Trinity Briana McBride was born on November 7th and transitioned on November 17th.

There's no poetic way to tell you that I died on the inside and felt every ounce of pain attached to such a loss. I'll never forget running into the emergency room with my daughter wrapped in a blanket, begging for help with a face full of tears. Shock set in as I watched the doctors and nurses scatter, doing everything they could. At the same time, I felt detached, like I was outside my body, watching myself hold my baby girl while her father and grandparents stood in the room after she was pronounced gone. In those first 60 seconds (or maybe less), a battle raged inside me: me vs. me. I told myself I wouldn't recover. I told myself life was over. I even told myself that God set me up. My mind simply couldn't accept that I was holding my lifeless baby. How could this be my life? What did I do to deserve this?

Everything I thought I knew about life, love, motherhood, and faith unraveled with the silence of my baby's heartbeat. That inner battle shifted. The 'me vs. me' moment transformed into something beyond myself—God and/or His angels versus me. This shift saved my life, though I must recommit to it whenever I drown in grief. That day I chose to live, not die. I know this may be hard for some to hear; still, it's my truth. The questions flooded back: How could I live or move forward without my baby? How am I supposed to function? I had no idea how I would navigate life. But I clung to the impulse to live for Trinity. I wanted to make her proud. Even in just 10 days, she brought immense joy to our families. She was loved beyond measure, but her work here was done.

SIDS — Sudden Infant Death Syndrome. A phrase I never expected to become my reality. A phrase that doesn't ease the pain or make any of it make sense. It doesn't tell you how it feels to plan a funeral instead of a first birthday. It doesn't speak of the guilt that haunts your every breath: Did I miss something? Did I fail her? It doesn't explain how her clothes still smelled like baby lotion and how I couldn't bring myself to wash them. Or how I kept hearing phantom cries in the night and jumping up, only to remember there was no baby to soothe. My boobs were still producing milk, but I had no baby to feed. No milestones. No first tooth, first step, or first word. They call it Sudden Infant Death Syndrome, but to me it was theft. One minute, she was alive and breathing, fine. The next she was gone, leaving behind a bassinet that would never get a chance to hold her again. There are no words strong enough to capture that moment: my baby wasn't coming back home.

The hours that followed were a blur: police, doctors, family, friends, funeral decisions, tears, silence. I remember feeling angry when the officers told me about their investigation and that they'd have to go to my home. They took Trinity's blanket (which I still don't have back). They also had my phone for over 24 hours. Though I understood it was protocol, I wish it had been trauma-informed. In such a traumatic moment, reality slipped away, and nothing seemed to make sense. The contrast between anticipation—a big gender reveal, two baby showers—and profound loss—no first birthday—struck me. I didn't just lose my daughter. I lost myself. No one tells you grief can be that paralyzing: life moves on while you are emotionally, mentally, and spiritually impaired.

When I made the decision to live and return to myself, I realized my next move had to be for my own long-term well-being or I would lose myself entirely. Reaching for help became my lifeline: I sent a text message to my therapist, and another to my mentor. I knew I couldn't get through this alone and needed my "anchors" more than ever. My therapist needed to know, as the person supporting my mental and emotional health, and my mentor's prayers and intuitive support were essential. I thank God I found the strength to think strategically when it mattered. Instead of spiraling deeper, I began the work of stepping out—sometimes all we can do is talk and walk ourselves forward.

As weeks passed, I existed in a fog. I performed life like a badly rehearsed role play I didn't audition for. People said all the "right" things: She's in a better place, God needed another Angel, it'll get better. Nothing triggered me more than "You can have another one." They didn't understand that Trinity and her memory could not be replaced. Her absence was not a hole to be patched up; it was a scar etched into my soul. While I knew most meant well, I wanted to scream. When meeting someone in their grief, it's better to say less and do more. Show up and be present. That's enough.

Grief is lonely. People surround you at first, offering food, hugs, and well-meaning words. But as weeks turned into months, I felt a new expectation to "move on." I sensed people wanted the old me back—the smiling, functioning version. What they missed is that Trinity died, but so did the version of me they knew. This loneliness is specific—a kind only grieving mothers understand. Time passes, but my calendar is stuck on the day my child died. I couldn't handle baby showers or kid parties. Even seeing a baby's photo online could shatter me. People talk about grief like a heavy blanket. For me, it was like being set on fire from the inside out. I was filled with anger and questions. I couldn't think, eat, enjoy things I used to enjoy, or barely talk. Most days my heart felt like it was ripped out of my chest. I went to see a cardiologist to make sure it was just grief. My doctor ordered multiple tests. Now that I think about it, I'm pretty sure she knew everything was okay. She scheduled testing for my own sanity. During one appointment, while looking at the chambers of my heart on the screen, I'll never forget that soft whisper that said, "I'm broken." I cried like a baby. The tech didn't know what to do or say, but she held me and let me get it out. I wish I could find her again. I would love to thank her for giving me that space. I wasn't sure if she read my chart and knew I just lost a baby or if she was just being who God needed her to be in that moment. Either way, I'm convinced angels surrounded me when I needed them the most.

I spent most nights wrestling with God. I cried, yelled, threw stuff, and had multiple meltdowns. I begged for answers. I cried until I had no tears left. I asked, "How could you take her from me? What kind of God lets a mother bury her child?" There were times I turned my back on him. Too angry to pray. Too wounded to sing. Yet, deep down, I still knew he was the only one who could carry me through this. My faith was not strong during those days. It was raw, messy, and filled with doubt. Even in my doubt, I clung to the tiniest shred of hope that he had not abandoned me completely. I was scared to take my questions, anger, sadness, and pain to him. Instead of talking to him, I stayed silent. I didn't begin talking to him until one of my friends texted me saying she wondered what my conversations with God were like. I told her they were nonexistent, and I had nothing to say. She told me that he understood and could handle every emotion I may bring. That day, I lost it in my room. It was just him and me. I told him I was angry. I told him I didn't deserve this and questioned why it was happening to me. I cried and cried. My room reflected the aftermath of a tornado when I was done, but it was the release I needed.

Before losing Trinity, I spent most of my life as a highly functioning depressive person whose anxiety made it hard to be open, vulnerable, or vocal about my needs. I'd been through so much, but you could never tell—I'd perfected my mask, always being everything for others and nothing for myself. After Trinity, the world itself felt foreign. I went back to work, hoping distraction would save me, but grief accompanied me everywhere. Upon returning, I learned I would be on the Grief and Traumatic Loss team—no conversation, just assigned after losing my daughter. That only deepened my spiral. Grief interrupted my work, pushing me out of meetings to cry. It followed me to the grocery store, making in-person shopping impossible. Instacart became my lifeline. Even trying to sleep, grief whispered to me. Simple tasks became overwhelming; I existed in my notes app, planning how to eat, shower, or just sit on the balcony. Pretending took everything from me. Ultimately, I broke. Suddenly, the mask no longer fit my face.

I was forced to sit in my pain, spend time with God, and pour into myself. During this time, I took a leave of absence from work and stepped away from outside responsibilities and roles. I spent time practicing the pause. Coming to terms with where I was and what I needed. Isolation, which I now know was solitude, saved my life. If I would have continued to ignore the fact that I was struggling, I'm not sure where I would be. I spent weeks doing intensive therapy, journaling, studying my bible, picking up new interests/hobbies, doubling down on self-care, rewiring my nervous system, allowing myself to feel without running from my pain, and learning this new version of me.

Eventually, the weight of grief collided with the harsh realities of life. Clinically, the psychiatrist I was seeing would not clear me to go back to work. I was okay with it until I began to suffer financially. I remember spending most of my day calling unemployment, literally calling 70 times back-to-back, because most days the phone would disconnect due to high call volume. On other days, I would finally get someone on the phone, only to have the call disconnect with no answers or guidance on my claim. In the midst of my frustration, all I could think about was trying to find a way to avoid grieving mothers from having to experience this. My car was repossessed, and I was in the process of losing my home. Eviction was another layer of humiliation and despair piled on top of my sorrow. People often assume grief is just emotional, but it seeps into every part of your life. I was drowning, not only in loss but in the practical consequences of being broken and unable to function. In this breaking, I surrendered to God. I told him I knew he would use this pain for something greater. That was the turning point. Not because everything suddenly became easier, but because I stopped trying to be in control. I stopped trying to fight grief on my own terms.

In true God fashion, he knew what I needed to keep going. He sent my rainbow after the storm, Serenity Sevyn. She gave me a reason to fight. Was it hard? Absolutely! I walked on eggshells my whole pregnancy, and if I'm honest, most days it felt hard to breathe. I made sure I had an emotional safety plan so both pain and happiness could exist in a healthy way. Holding her for the first time was both healing and terrifying. Every cough, every nap, every quiet moment triggered memories of what I had lost, her big sister. But Serenity taught me to live again. She reminded me that love is not canceled by loss, that my heart was capable of holding both grief and joy. Parenting after loss is not simple. It is layered with anxiety, tenderness, and a profound awareness of life's fragility. Serenity has been a light in the darkness, a living reminder that God still writes new stories after devastation.

From sitting in solitude, The Purpose Ark (TPA) was born. It didn't come to me fully formed; it started as a whisper, a vision of turning my pain into a lifeboat for others drowning in their own sorrows. I wanted no other mother to feel as alone as I felt. I began connecting with other grieving mothers, collaborating on events and workshops to promote healing, and being transparent about my own story and my journey. I even joined the Star Legacy Foundation as a peer companion to connect with mothers across the country who are experiencing the same pain. And slowly, I stopped feeling like a graveyard. I started feeling like a garden – not the well-kept kind, but the wild kind, where beautiful things grow from ashes and untamed soil. There was this strong sense of purpose, determination, and empowerment to do what I know God called me to do. With TPA, I commit to being a trauma and mental health advocate, as well as a grief coach. I will create brave spaces for people to share their stories without judgment. I built TPA not because I was healed, but because I was still in the process of healing. It was my way of reminding myself—and others—that even the most shattered lives can be rebuilt into something purposeful. The truth is, you don't get over losing a child. Grief doesn't end; it changes shapes. Some days it's a sharp stab; other days it's a dull ache, but it never disappears. What changed is me. I no longer see grief as my enemy. It is not my companion, a reminder of the depth of my love for Trinity.

...I stopped feeling like a graveyard.

I started feeling like a garden.

Carrying her memory forward is part of who I am. I laugh, I love, and I have been able to dream again – but always with her name stitched into the fabric of my being. One of the biggest lies grief tells us is that the love we gave, the love we felt, ends with the person's last breath. But Trinity taught me otherwise. She taught me that love transcends time. That I could mother a child in death. That her life, though short, had infinite meaning. She made me unafraid to look pain in the eye. She made me want to live, not just survive — so I could carry her name into the spaces that needed it most. Grief is not a chapter I'll ever close. But it is one I've learned to read aloud now. To say, This is me. Broken and beautiful. Wounded and wise. Still healing, still hurting, but moving forward with purpose. This chapter may have started in grief, but it ends in love.

To the Grieving Mother Reading This

If you've ever lost a child — in the womb, in the world, or in your arms — I see you.

I know the weight you carry.

I know the ache that never fully leaves.

And I want you to know: you are still a mother. You still matter. Your child still matters.

You don't have to "move on." But you can move forward — at your pace, in your way.

And if the world tells you to be silent, to "get over it," I hope you scream their name louder. I hope you find your version of purpose. Whether it's a book, a tattoo, a support group, a song, a prayer, an intentional period of isolation, or a breath — you get to decide what their legacy looks like.

Public Service Awareness: SIDS Awareness & Safe Sleep

- **Always place babies on their backs to sleep.**
- **Keep cribs free of toys, pillows, and blankets.**
- **Share awareness, save a life — every conversation counts.**

Meet the Author - Lisa Tyson

My name is Lisa L Carter and I am a proud mother of two young adults, Taylor (26) and Robert (21). My motto to them has always been: you will succeed in spite of your hardships, not fail because of them.

I am an adventurer by nature. I enjoy working out at the gym. I create positive environments where people can learn and thrive. I choose laughter in most cases. I am grateful for each day that I get to spend on God's green earth with my children and family.

Professionally, I am a Program Manager in the social service field. I have been with the Center for Family Services for 20 years. My work centers on helping others. I am also a master-level, professionally trained vocalist. I have been singing since I was three years old. I sing a wide range of genres, including country, R&B, and opera. My favorite is inspirational music. I have been a worship leader and music director for what seems like forever. Singing and uplifting people is one of my purposes.

When I leave a room, it should be better than when I entered it!

Anchor Word: Tenacity

Paula's Prelude

Some stories whisper survival — Lisa's *sings* it. Her journey reminds us that faith does not erase pain; it carries us through it. Each loss could have silenced her song, but instead, it deepened her sound. Her testimony is a melody of tenacity — proof that grace not only sustains, it strengthens.

Grief is layered. Just when one ache settles, another surfaces — yet with each unveiling, grace gives us strength to rise again.

Through it all, I survived

Anchor Word: Tenacity

I often struggle to capture my experiences with grief and loss. The best place to begin seems to be at the beginning.

Let me share a bit about where I come from. I grew up in Somerdale, New Jersey, but my family's roots are in Bowman and Orangeburg, South Carolina. My mother, Loretta Glover Wells, left Bowman to move north and leave the cotton fields behind. My grandfather was a sharecropper and a pastor. My father, Reverdy Ransom Wells Sr., is from Summerton, South Carolina. He played an important part in the "Griggs vs. Elliot" case, which helped start "Brown vs. Board of Education." With a family history like this, you might think my life would be easy. However, grief soon found me alongside any successes.

When I was 9 years old, one of my favorite television shows was "Tarzan." One particular afternoon, I tried to make a tire swing, using a rope my father had already tied around a large limb at the top of a tree in our backyard. I had big ideas for swinging from the tree, but looking back, my plans were not well thought out. During my first attempt, I tied the rope around my left arm, then my waist, and finally my neck. I did not intend any harm to myself. I was just a child at play, not thinking about the consequences. As I hung from the tree with the rope around my neck, slight panic set in. Fortunately, my father looked out his bedroom window at that moment. He saw me hanging by my neck from the tree as if I had lynched myself. My father cut me down with the pocket knife he always carried. Afterward, my parents vowed never to give me another rope—whether for play or anything else. They kept that promise until the day they died. Despite the scare, ***I survived.***

A couple of years later, around age 11, another incident tested my resilience. Ignoring my mother's warning, I set out to walk to a nearby store. Upon my return, a car pulled up, blocking my way home. A man demanded that I get in, and when I refused, he tried to grab me. I narrowly escaped and ran home, but the man was never found. Even then, ***I survived.*** Years passed, and as I entered my teenage years, loss became an even more tangible part of my life. At 16, my grandmother died suddenly. Soon after, my uncle died, then my father's only sister. My grandfather died before I was born. That year, two classmates took their own lives. After a brief pause in my losses following high school, grief returned once I graduated from college. In my mid-twenties, I faced a new wave: my grandmother died, followed by my uncle, my first cousin's triplet, my first cousin (the triplet's mother), and my mother's best friend.

Even with all the loss, there were happy times too. When I was 23, I met and married Robert Neil Carter. Two years later, we had our first child, Taylor Carter. I named her Taylor Lillian after my grandmother, Lillian Glover, who passed away while I was pregnant. My husband and I only dated for nine months before getting married, but it worked out for us. My mother was overjoyed because Taylor was the first granddaughter in our family. But that happiness didn't last long. When my daughter was only three months old, my mother was diagnosed with colon cancer. I remember sitting in the waiting room, holding my baby, when the doctor told us it was stage 4 and my mother might only have six months to live. She passed away just three months later. Losing her was the hardest thing I've ever faced. It felt like the person who loved me most was gone, and I was completely alone. Still, ***I survived.***

No one really talks about the feelings you have to work through with God.

Every time, I found a way to keep going, but I have to admit I was angry with God. I was 26, married, with a six-month-old daughter, but I felt completely alone. No one really talks about the feelings you have to work through with God. My family was full of pastors, and I had been singing in church since I was three. At that time, I was a worship leader. But none of that kept me from feeling hurt by God. I remember thinking, 'God, I've praised you for years, and the only thing I asked was for you to save my mother, but you didn't.' Those thoughts were normal, even if they weren't right. They felt more real than anything else.

Now, the music and songs I once loved only gave me pain. The songs I sang to uplift others became unbearable to me. I had to spend time in honest conversations with God to recover from the pain. Losing my mother was like living with two arms and waking up with one. You spend your life learning to function with that one arm. In your heart, you miss and reminisce about life with two arms. You wonder how much better you would be if you were whole again. People say things like "God does not put more on you than you can bear," or "the person is in a better place." All of that may be true, but at that moment, it sounded like blah, blah, blah. Sometimes it's better to just tell a grieving person, "I am sorry and I love you." Although I felt in conflict with God, I sang one of those uplifting songs at my mother's funeral. ***I survived.***

Time moved on. Fast forward to 2006, seven years after my mother died in 1999. That year, my father was diagnosed with congestive heart failure. My son, Robert Jaylen Carter II, had been born about a year and a half earlier, in 2004. My father passed away suddenly on Thanksgiving in 2006. I was 34 and felt like an orphan. Singing at his funeral brought back all the pain from my mother's funeral. But once again, ***I survived***.

Seven months later, on July 29, 2007, my husband Rob left early for the 7:30 a.m. church service because he was playing on an adult basketball team. He had been my biggest support since my parents died. Around 9:00 a.m., while my son and I were heading to our own church service, Rob called to say he was on his way to his game. He told me he loved me and that he'd see me later. After church, my phone rang. It was Rob's number, but a voice I didn't know asked if I was Rob Carter's wife. I said yes. The man told me Rob had passed out while playing basketball and was on his way to the emergency room. He also said he wasn't sure if Rob was breathing when he left in the ambulance. Hearing that made me deeply worried.

When I got to the emergency room, I saw Rob being taken out of the ambulance while they did CPR. They rushed him past me, still doing chest compressions. I told them I was his wife, but they asked me to wait in the waiting room. While I waited, I called family and friends to ask for prayers, because I was raised in the church and truly believe in prayer. But I learned that prayer can't always change God's will or plans, even if we don't understand them at the time. Soon, the doctor called me into a room alone and told me that my husband of almost 11 years, the father of our two young children, had died. A blood clot had stopped his heart. This happened in July 2007, seven years after my mother died and seven months after my father passed. Spiritually, the number 7 is often seen as a symbol of completion or perfection. It didn't feel that way to me, but I had to trust God.

Losing my husband was a pain I had never known before. What hurt most was not being able to protect my two children from it. I didn't know how to comfort them when I couldn't even comfort myself. My daughter Taylor was in South Carolina with family, her first time away from home. Telling her what happened when she returned was almost unbearable. My family came up from South Carolina right away. I could always count on my uncles, aunts, and first cousins, who felt more like siblings, to support me. My brother Reverdy Jr and spiritual brother Tom Chamberlain were also there for me. Sadly, my middle brother Jason and I were not close at that time, but that's another story for another time. When Taylor came home, I had to tell her about her father. It's still the hardest thing I've ever had to do. She walked in, hugged me, and asked, 'Where's Daddy?' I started to cry and told her he had gone to heaven. The look on her face still haunts me today. Later, my son, who was almost three, asked, 'Why would God take Daddy to heaven when I need him here with me?' I told him that he was in Heaven with God. I sang at my husband's funeral to show my children, Taylor and Robert, and my bonus children, Devante and Daja, that we would get through this.

I had to trust God because He was all I had left. My parents and my husband were gone. People don't talk much about the emptiness that only God can fill, or the deep pain of missing someone's touch and presence every night. Being a one-income family brought its own challenges. Not being able to protect my children from losing their father, and feeling helpless about it, was a heavy burden. Even so, I had to keep them focused on God, even though the hurt was indescribable. Sleep stopped being restful and became a reminder of what I had lost. But ***I survived.***

Almost exactly four months later, I was in South Carolina with my family, seeking some peace in the life I now had. It was my cousin Vikki's husband's birthday. Everyone called him 'Man,' though his real name was Arthur. I tried to change my flight to join his birthday celebration, but it didn't work out, so I sent my well wishes the night before and went home. Later, my cousin called to tell me that Vikki and Man had been hit by a drunk driver that night, and Man didn't survive. It was hard to believe that both of us—first cousins, both in our early thirties, both with two young children, both orphans—were now widows too. I returned to South Carolina to support Vikki and her children through what felt like an endless hardship. I wish I had something wise or comforting to say to her, but I didn't, even though our lives always seemed to parallel. All I could say was that we would get through it together, just like we always had.

My Uncle Chris told me it might be too much for me to sing at Man's funeral since losing my husband was still so fresh. But with God's help, I sang anyway. God gave me clear instructions: stand right in front of Vikki while I sang. I told God I didn't think I could handle seeing pain I knew so well. As I tried to sing 'The Battle is the Lord's' by Yolanda Adams, I felt a struggle inside me that no one else could see. God told me to stop singing and let Him sing for me. I argued in my mind, thinking I couldn't just stop in the middle of a song. Looking back, it makes me smile that I thought I could argue with God. But suddenly, I forgot every word and stood silent in front of everyone. People could see I was struggling. It felt like I had two voices in my head—one telling me to walk away and say I couldn't do it, that it was too much. People would have understood, since it had only been four months since my husband died. But then I felt God telling me again, 'Let me sing this for you.' So I opened my mouth and sang, though I barely remember how I finished. Afterward, I walked back to my seat, barely able to breathe. In that moment, I realized God gave us exactly what we needed. The family needed Him. But yet again ***I survived.***

You might expect that after all this, life would get easier. But that didn't happen. I lost another first cousin, my cousin's triplet, two uncles, three grandparents, my cousin's son, and more family and friends than I can count. All of this was in addition to losing my parents and my husband. We kept facing loss after loss. Still, ***I survived***.

More recently, in 2025, I went through a divorce after eight years of marriage. Divorce is its own kind of loss, but that's a story for another day too. Then I faced another heartbreak. My cousin Jade, who was like a sister to me, died unexpectedly at 38. She was the light of our family—vibrant, funny, with blue eyes and a golden heart. Professionally, she was Dr. Jade, PhD. My daughter looked just like her physically and on the basketball court. Losing her was almost impossible to understand. At her funeral, I said, 'I don't know how we'll go on without Jade, but I know God will heal our hearts, just like He always does.' I sang a medley of songs at Jade's funeral. I remembered how she used to joke with me before I sang, saying, 'You better not mess up,' and then she'd laugh. Afterward, she'd tease me, 'You didn't have to do all that up there.' You might think grief gets easier as you get older and wiser, but it doesn't. But ***I survived.***

I've shared all of this for a reason, not to make you feel sorry for me or focus on sadness. I want to remind you that God always has a purpose for what you go through.

You might not see it when you're in the middle of grief, but looking back, you learn more from your pain than you realize. I've had other losses too, but I shared what mattered most for this story. What I want you to know is that ***I survived.*** My story started with sadness, but it ends with peace, happiness, and a renewed love for God. God showed Himself to me in ways I never would have known without these losses. Most of all, He showed me that He can heal a broken heart. It's painful, and sometimes you're not okay, but in the end, you will be. Just like me, you can find peace, experience joy, and love again in ways you can't imagine.

If you're just starting your journey, know that this is what the bible calls "A light affliction" in 2nd Corinthians 4:17. I remember my spiritual brother Tom told me that after the loss of my husband that my situation was "a light affliction," which upset me at first. But now I understand what he meant. A light affliction doesn't mean your burden feels light, but it means it's temporary. It means that the weight that you are carrying won't last forever.

That's why I ended each story about loss with, "**But I survived.**" I did that on purpose. My losses allowed God to reveal Himself to me. I had always heard about who people said God was. But until you are in a situation for yourself, you will never know your own strength or the undeniable goodness of God. Life is unpredictable, full of ups and downs. But the hard times aren't meant to defeat you—allow them to better you with God's help. My Aunt Priscilla said something profound to me after we lost her daughter, my sister/1st cousin Dr. Jade. She said, "The only difference between a stepping stone and a stumbling block is how high you lift your foot." I'm not saying this journey is easy. But I am grateful that God made me who I am.

There's only one you in this world. You are special, and no matter what you go through, keep lifting your foot high and know that you will survive—because ***I survived.***

Sometimes strength doesn't roar — it rests. Healing is the quiet courage to keep showing up even when the story still stings.

Meet the Author - Ronaldlyn Latham

Ronaldlyn Latham, affectionately known as Ronnie among family, friends, and colleagues, resides in Southern NJ. She was married for 32 years until she was widowed. She is a mother of two—her daughter is 39 years old, and her son, who has passed away, is in heaven. Ronaldlyn graduated from Strayer University in March 2022 with a Bachelor's degree in Criminal Justice. She is a federal public servant, recently marking 23 years of service. Ronaldlyn is a member of The Perfecting Church, where she volunteers with Loving Our Cities and leads the Mending Hearts Ministry, supporting mothers who have experienced the devastating loss of a child.

Ronaldlyn is the visionary author of "Gracefully Broken, Beautifully Restored," an anthology of hope and healing written by thirteen grieving mothers. She is also the author of "Love, Lust, and Starting Again: A Spiritual Guide for Dating After Losing a Spouse," which is dedicated to her husband.

Ronaldlyn's mission is to help mothers heal by providing love, hope, and support during difficult times. Drawing from personal experience, she lost both her husband and her son, tragedies that changed her life and inspired her mission of healing. After three years of counseling and spiritual growth since these losses, she continues her journey of restoration.

Anchor Word: Transformation

Paula's Prelude

Ronnie's story is the kind of testimony that only time and truth can tell. Her journey through compounded grief—losing both her son and husband within two weeks—reveals the courage it takes to live again after unimaginable pain. What stands out most is her willingness to be honest about the anger, confusion, and silence that accompany grief, while still choosing faith as her anchor. Her transformation reminds us that grace does not erase pain; it rebuilds what was shattered, one surrendered moment at a time.

✨ Pause & Proceed

Every story of loss teaches us how to love better. The lessons we learn in sorrow often become the language we speak in service.

The Beauty after the Broken: A Journey of Transformation

Anchor Word: Transformation

My name is Ronaldlyn Latham, and I am fondly known to all friends, family, and colleagues as Ronnie. I am a 60-year-old widow. I am a mother, daughter, sister, aunt, and friend. I have a daughter who is 39 and a son in heaven. My husband, Rodney A. Latham, died suddenly on January 3, 2017, after 32 years of marriage. My rock, partner, chef, and love of my life is gone.

Rodney and I both grew up in Philadelphia on Price Street, just a block away from each other. He always liked me, but I thought of him as just a neighborhood friend. We went to camp together, and his brother would often talk about him. One time, Rodney paid for my movie ticket, but I ended up sitting with another guy I liked, who also happened to be named Rodney.

Rodney was two years older than me. After high school, he graduated with honors and joined the U.S. Navy. When he visited, we would catch up. One time, he asked me to open my trench coat. When he saw my belly, he realized I was pregnant. Rodney joked, "You had to be fast in the behind, didn't you. You couldn't wait for me?" He rubbed my belly and said the baby should have been his. I didn't know what to say. I gave birth to my son, Jakeith Kaheed Brown (later Latham), on April 19, 1982, and sent Rodney a birth announcement while he was on the USS Nimitz. He got it three months later. At that time, he was stationed in Jacksonville, Florida, and living with a girlfriend. One night, he had a dream that he believed was from God, telling him to go home and get his wife. He drove 14 hours back to Philadelphia to claim me as his wife, even though we had never been on a date. Our first date was at his family reunion, where he introduced me as his girlfriend. We dated through my senior year and got married on May 19, 1984.

Have you ever thought that when one event happens, it's all downhill from there? In November 2016, my husband fell outside and injured his head, and didn't tell anyone. The next day, he fell out of bed having a seizure and was rushed to Kennedy Hospital (now known as Jefferson) to have emergency brain surgery. He had a brain bleed. God successfully brought Rodney through that surgery and our family was there to support him during his recovery and rehabilitation. Our son, Jakeith, spent more time with his dad than my daughter and me because we both had to work. Jakeith was self-employed and set his own hours, allowing him to be present for his dad during the day at the hospital and during rehabilitation.

Rodney worked hard during rehabilitation, focused on returning home and to work. Unfortunately, returning to work was not an option. As we began to navigate the changes this new chapter brought, Rodney was not the same after brain surgery. He was discharged from rehab and came home on December 16, 2016. Life seemed to be going okay.

Rodney was home, and my employer let me work from home so I could care for him. The kids were very attentive to their dad and his needs. I thanked God for this miracle and believed our family would get through it. However, everything changed. On December 20, 2016, our son Jakeith was murdered in New Castle County, Delaware, during a robbery, and my world fell apart. Exactly two weeks after Jakeith died, my husband passed away in our bedroom on January 3, 2017. The doctors called it broken heart syndrome.

Yes, there is such a thing. As shock and grief took hold, my husband blamed himself for not being with our son the day he was murdered. He kept replaying the narrative in his head and couldn't accept that someone had killed our son while he wasn't there to protect him. My husband was always the family protector. Not being there for our son shattered him, and it broke his heart. As a result, I was in deep shock and stricken with grief myself. My first thought was, this cannot be real—God, you must be punking me. Suddenly, I was facing another funeral to plan while still dealing with our son's loss. In those days, I didn't know what to feel or think, only that I had lost both my son and husband within two weeks. My sorrow turned to anger toward my husband for leaving me.

It may sound harsh, but my anger over Rodney leaving me was overwhelming, and I wanted to erase him. In this state, I deleted his Facebook page, which made my daughter angry. She accused me of erasing her dad, and now I regret that decision deeply.

I was suddenly alone for the first time since I was nineteen, forced to navigate life as a widow and single. I had to ask for help—something I rarely did during 32 years of marriage. With my daughter by my side, the loneliness and anger persisted. My anger stemmed from losing both our son and Rodney. I had always thought Rodney and I would grow old together. He was our protector, making me feel safe. At nineteen, I had experienced unconditional love—a love that thrived on family, sacrifice, and shared meals. Rodney was happiest when family gathered to enjoy his cooking.

I remember when I was pregnant with our daughter. The day she was born he beamed with joy and happiness. He looked down at her little face with adoration. For Rodney, the U.S. Navy was not his greatest accomplishment; creating our daughter was. He loved her with everything he had in him. She was his Lil Baby.

Losing Rodney changed me. I realized how much I relied on him. I took his presence for granted after 32 years of marriage. I never expected he could be gone in a moment. I struggled with not knowing how to do CPR. I desperately called 9-1-1 for help. When paramedics arrived, I asked if he was breathing. I was told he was not on his own. I expected the hospital would save him, but that was not the case. I was isolated while he was treated. I learned his heart had stopped and could not be restarted. I lost control and screamed. I was allowed to see Rodney, who looked as if he was sleeping. His sister told him to wake up. Our daughter, stunned, asked Pastor Kevin Brown, 'What kind of God would do this?' Pastor Kevin had no words for my daughter in that moment. As I write this, I am tearing up. That reality hit me like a ton of bricks. On January 3, 2017, I woke up a wife. By 12:00 noon, I was a widow.

Losing Rodney has changed every part of who I am, and I carry the weight of his words with me every day. His absence is felt in every challenge faced alone and every joy I wish I could share with him. Yet, as I reflect on our family's journey—enduring love, profound loss, unyielding grief, and hard-won resilience—I choose to honor both Rodney and Jakeith by living with hope. Their love strengthens me. Even though the path forward can feel lonely, I move ahead, one step at a time, allowing their influence to guide me toward new beginnings. I am not defined by loss, but uplifted by love that endures.

During grief, I felt angry and alone, unaware that others noticed my pain. Members of my church and friends encouraged me to seek help. Regina Egerton from my pCell small group at The Perfecting Church noticed my anger and referred me to counseling, which allowed me to process my emotions for four years. Minister Angela Brown later connected me to the Mending Hearts Ministry, which became the catalyst for my healing. I learned to let go of anger and bitterness, allowing God to reshape me inside and out. Looking at old pictures, I barely recognized myself. My transformation began the day my husband passed away.

Although the deepest shift began when our son was murdered, I realized I was no longer the person I had been for 32 years. As this grief journey unfolded, a new me started to emerge—a person unfamiliar even to myself. A friend compared me to a butterfly: she said I was a caterpillar in a cocoon, but that, in time, a beautiful butterfly would appear. I wondered what beauty, if any, could come from such trauma. Nothing I learned in 32 years of marriage prepared me for this compounded grief. Although I believe in God, I felt no comfort during church sermons and scripture readings. I also grappled with everyday losses—no one to put my cold feet on at night, to shop, to cook, to fix things, or to provide a sense of protection. My thoughts spiraled with questions: Why did this happen? Was I being punished? Could I have changed the outcome? I rehashed everything constantly for three years. Out of loneliness, I tried dating a year and a half after my husband passed, seeking a connection with a man. That attempt underscored just how much had changed—for me, it did not work out.

The grief journey taught me so many things I did not know. Like there are five stages of grief: denial, anger, bargaining, depression, and acceptance, and there is no time frame for how long you can be in any of the stages. I experienced some of these stages at once. The grief journey is not easy, and you should not travel it alone. You can't heal by isolating from others and waiting for the old you to return. I was no longer the Ronnie I had been comfortable with all those years. Every emotion I felt was real, and I felt like I was losing my mind. During my journey through grief I lost friends and family, people who I thought would be there for support were not. Married friends and family definitely abandoned me because I was no longer a wife. Things that I was passionate about, I lost interest in. I was an avid reader, but now reading seems to be a chore, rather than something I enjoy. Transformation was taking place before I recognized what was happening. Losing my husband was not something I expected, but I had to find a way to get out of this dark place I was in. You see, I learned you can visit the dark place, but you can't stay there. Staying there leaves you depressed, angry, and alone. I wanted things to go back to the way they were.

...you can visit the dark place, but you can't stay there. Staying there leaves you depressed, angry, and alone.

Not possible at all. I learned that I was not alone on this journey and met other women who lost their spouses. I understand the loneliness and the wondering of what you will do with your life now. I have experienced the absence of my husband in a way no one will understand unless you have been married as long as I have or longer. Yes, there is a void and emptiness in your heart that feels like it can never be filled. All emotions and feelings are valid, and grieving has no time limit. You can experience happiness, sadness, anger, and crying all in the same day. I knew I needed help, and I am an advocate for counseling or therapy. Some people may think it doesn't help, but crying and talking through it is therapeutic. Counseling and Mending Heart Ministry were a safe place for me to share my feelings. There was no judgment, just me being raw and transparent about how I felt.

I began to talk to God more and read the bible and transformation was taking place. I speak to him as I would to a good friend. I screamed, yelled, and poured out my broken heart to him. I wanted this loneliness and emptiness to go away. I wanted to live again, but I didn't know how. That's why it's beneficial to know that others are on the same journey, allowing you to support one another. Love, support, and hope are what moved me toward my healing and transformation. I no longer saw the loss of my husband as a bad thing anymore. I have learned to accept what God allowed, which was the hardest thing I had to do. I now thank God for 32 years of marriage. I thank God for my husband's unconditional love. I thank God for the time he allowed me to be loved, supported, and protected by my husband. Grief took me to a place of gratefulness. When I see pictures of my husband, I smile. My thoughts are happy when I reflect on our life. It was 32 years of growing together, loving each other, raising our children, and being present for one another. Rodney Latham is resting until we meet again, and until then, I will continue to speak his name and hold him in my heart.

I pray that as you read my testimony of grief and gratitude, you will hear and see the transformation that took place in my life through the grace of God. I could not navigate to the other side of grief without God being there every step of the way. I stand on 2 Kings 20:5: 'I have heard your prayers and have seen your tears; I will heal you.' My transformation brought about a change in my walk with God and my faith, and I know personally that He is close to the broken-hearted and He binds their wounds.

Meet the Author - Martin Hollis, Jr

Martin Hollis, Jr, aka "MJ", is a devoted husband, father, and son whose creative reflections bridge generations. A middle school history teacher with a passion for politics, debate, and anime, he writes with quiet strength and introspective depth. Through honesty and reverence, MJ explores what it means to inherit values, carry legacy, and forge identity after loss – inviting readers to see grief not as an ending, but as an invitation to grow forward.

Anchor Word: Forward-Thinking

Paula's Prelude

Grief doesn't just look back—it looks ahead. MJ's reflection reveals the tension between honoring what we've inherited and becoming who we're meant to be. His words remind us that forward-thinking is not about leaving the past behind but about carrying legacy with intention, allowing love and responsibility to evolve as we do.

When the Understudy becomes the Lead

Anchor Word: Forward-thinking

Have you ever been haunted by the vivid replay of moments with someone you've lost? Sometimes, these memories surface unexpectedly as you navigate your daily life. Have you wished for just a fleeting chance—mere seconds—to hear their voice again or to ask for advice?

Seeking moments of reflection, or echoes, about the ones we've lost becomes part of daily life. These echoes might be captured in a photograph, stashed in an album, or stored in a gallery on your phone. A video showing them in their element can also serve as a moment of nostalgia. Sharing their stories at events or small gatherings is a way to keep their presence alive. These stories help children understand what life was like when that person was still around. There's a desire to maintain their memory and prevent their life from disappearing into the past.

However, grief often brings with it a weightier burden: the legacy and responsibilities that are left behind. This weight of inheritance is what consumes my thoughts during moments of reflection. Suddenly, you find yourself in a position where you have to carry forward traditions, values, and roles. This mantle of responsibility, whether as the head of a family or the guardian of the next generation, is something that I find particularly daunting as I think about my father's passing.

At the same time, there is the gift of guidance left by those we've lost. The values and lessons they shared shape us, but they also offer a choice—how much of their legacy do we aspire to continue, and how much do we allow ourselves to forge our own paths? This balance of carrying forth a legacy while choosing our path is where fresh insights often emerge, particularly as I find myself at this crossroads after losing my father.

When my father died, my mind turned to my son. Would he recall the special moments they shared, like wearing my father's hat and waiting for him to come home from work? At that time, my son was his only grandchild; I am still the only one in my immediate family with a child, guiding the next generation forward. I ask myself: What will my son's future hold without his grandfather? And beyond that, whose legacy am I living for—mine or my father's? Many people say they live on for those who have passed, but what does that really mean? Am I expected to act more like them, to fill their role? It's like being an understudy suddenly thrust on stage—the audience awaits, but you're not the original. Am I expected to fill the same role as before or create a new one? I didn't feel ready. Yet, it is important to recognize that feeling unprepared or uncertain is entirely natural. The journey of handling grief and legacy is fraught with doubts, and it's okay not to have all the answers right away. Even in uncertainty, we slowly forge a path forward, growing into the roles that we find ourselves in.

The journey of handling grief and legacy is fraught with doubts, and it's okay not to have all the answers right away.

Now, I always knew there would come a day when my Dad would no longer be around. Everyone mentally prepares themselves, at least a little bit, for that inevitability. I had steeled myself for that day, but I would be remiss if I didn't admit that I always envisioned a future where my Dad would be beside me, helping along the way. These hopes framed much of my thinking about family and legacy. In a perfect world, my son would be a little older, and my Dad would be able to see him grow up and have a child of his own. He would be there with me as I reached my next milestone: becoming a grandfather myself. That was a lofty dream I had, but it felt so much like my reality. I always remember my Dad saying how long-lived we are in my family. The uncles and aunts around me always seemed bigger than life. We would have these family gatherings where everyone always seemed so joyous and full of life. In my eyes, there was no way my Dad wouldn't make it to a hundred, as he had told me. Heck, I could see almost all my uncles and aunts making it to at least 90 years old. When my Dad was around, I felt more confident. I could continue to fail or take risks more assuredly because I knew my Dad had my back. In my life, I always felt like the odd man out: the one who failed or was considered weird. I'd often be too scared to move because I didn't want to embarrass myself, but more importantly, I didn't want to embarrass my family.

I often say, "I'm a Hollis. I need to carry myself like one." I placed more weight on my family name than my own, and after my father passed, I finally felt the legacy I needed to protect. Now, I am still a reflection of my parents' guidance, but if I fail, are people looking at just me or at my whole family? Since my Dad's passing, I've pushed myself to try new things, though I feel fear and uncertainty. My heart races, and my palms sweat with every new venture, yet I keep going. However, it's essential to remember that it's perfectly normal to feel this way. Honoring our legacy includes caring for ourselves, and allowing room for mistakes is part of that journey. Still, thinking of my father brings comfort. A gentle warmth spreads across my chest, even as a single tear rolls down my cheek.

Most people with this feeling can see this as a sign that they can do it and are on the right track. I observe a lot before making a move. That even includes moments before my father's passing. The moments I spent with my Dad were often spent in observation – watching how he handled himself in different situations, how he would quietly provide for and take care of us. He would let us struggle just a little, then come to us with a Bible verse or some encouragement to help us out of the situation. I found it corny back then, but somehow, I do the same thing with my son. My Dad had the hugest role to play in my life and in so many other people's. At his funeral, the number of people whose character and words my Dad had touched was astounding. The thing is, my Dad was just being himself. He wasn't perfect, but he lived his life to the best of his ability. My father often talked about his parents and how he wished they could see him now. He felt their absence and expectations, as I now feel his.

I am like my father in many ways, and I'm sure you, too, carry the flaws and victories of those who came before you. These inherited traits shape us into who we are today. Over the years, many have remarked on how much I resemble my father. His absence brings a bittersweet smile when I hear those comparisons. It's comforting yet poignant to know people see him in me. This realization can be incredibly joyful, as many of us cherish being likened to those we hold dear. Such reflections serve as a poignant reminder to propel our own stories forward. When the path is set before us, we need to walk it. We must be prepared for what comes, carrying lessons from their lives. We should strive to emulate their good works, remembering all the times shared. Then, in that shared journey, we can become the next evolution, both for ourselves and in memory of them.

As you reflect, consider whose footsteps you will follow. Which parts of the legacy left to you will you carry forward, and how will you make them your own? This journey invites us all to look forward and continue the traditions while crafting our unique identities.

✨ Pause & Proceed

**Legacy is not left — it is lived.
Every generation is a reflection
of the love that preceded it.**

Meet the Author - Maxwell Hollis

Maxwell Hollis (He/Him) is a 20-year-old multi-hyphenated artist from South Jersey. His craft includes writing, directing, acting, singing, and performing in numerous other capacities. Max attends Montclair State University, where he is expected to get his Bachelor of Arts in Theatre Studies. In his storytelling, he aims to engage audiences critically and encourage them to think beyond themselves. He believes true human development and connection begin there. Max holds these values close and hopes to keep creating and collaborating in spaces that challenge the human mind. When taking a break from his craft, Max enjoys playing piano and spending time with family and friends.

Connect with Max on Instagram @maxhollis20 or www.maxwellhollis.com

---

Anchor Word: Growth

Paula's Prelude

Sometimes grief doesn't arrive through death – it comes in the quiet surrender of dreams we've outgrown. In *Grief of Yourself*, Max explores the bittersweet art of letting go of one version of himself to make space for another. His story reminds us that identity, like purpose, is not fixed – it evolves with grace, grit, and growth.

When wisdom passes through generations, it becomes inheritance — not of wealth, but of worth.

Grief of Yourself

Anchor Word: Growth

Death and Grief are no strangers to me. I often joke with my friends and family that I have been to more funerals than I have weddings. I've even attended my own father's funeral right after turning sixteen years old. Still to this day, I mourn his death and him not being able to watch me grow up. However, this isn't the story I want to reflect on. It's the idea of how I am going to live my life going further without him.

To better understand my journey, it helps to know that I am a massive theatre nerd. I've participated in choir, show choir, and community theatre. Hell, I went to a vocational high school just to study theatre and joined the International Thespian Society, shoutout Troupe 5480! All of this is to say that I love the stage and the joy that performing brings me. Even going further, I am a plus-sized, black male in theatre, and being from a small town in South Jersey, everyone knew me. I was always known as the black guy who could actually dance, despite his weight, which is a backhanded compliment, but I digress. I was eager to break boundaries with this, and I wanted to prove myself in higher education.

However, things took a turn during my fall semester of senior year. I entered a very depressive state, which, of course, is the same time as application season. All of my friends were submitting their early applications to big arts schools like Ithaca and Carnegie Mellon, but for me, I was still trying to pass my English class. I often struggle with trying to prove myself too much as well. During the same time, I was treasurer of my Thespian society, working a part-time job, rehearsing for both an outside cabaret and my senior play, all while trying to start filming my prescreens. Prescreens are virtual auditions that occur before you can audition for a theatre school, which is common for schools that offer a Bachelor of Fine Arts (BFA) degree. To add to the stress, every school is different in what it wants from you. So, to say I was stressed truly was an understatement.

Despite these challenges, I ultimately submitted prescreens to only two schools: Rowan University and Montclair State University. Rowan was simply a safety, and they were more of a school that wanted me more than I wanted them. However, I fell in love with Montclair State. Being in-state, I was still close to home, but also wasn't literally next door. The theatre program was fantastic, and even better, it offered in-state tuition, which was ironic since I had claimed I would never attend a school in New Jersey. I submitted my prescreen for the Musical Theatre track that the school offered, which is actually one of the top 15 theatre schools in the country. This was now the perfect opportunity to prove I can make a career out of performing.

I was accepted into the University, but I still needed to be accepted into the Musical Theatre program. I ended up passing my pre-screen and was able to schedule an in-person audition with the school's faculty. I was one step closer to proving I can do this not only to others but to myself. By the spring of my high school senior year, my classmates and I were preparing for auditions at schools like Juilliard, Carnegie Mellon, and the University of Michigan. However, comparison is the thief of joy, which led me to focus on myself. On the day of my audition, I walked into Life Hall, the theatre hall of Montclair State, and couldn't help but see that there wasn't a single other black person in that building besides me. This was no stranger to me; it just gave me more incentive to strive for greatness. The day went on with me having to sing and act first, followed by a jazz dance. Now, I am a good dancer and can move, but genuinely, that dance was one of the hardest things I have ever had to do. Overall, I was ok with my audition. It wasn't my best, but I have performed worse. At the end of the auditioning day, they informed us that they would be sending out the results of our auditions within the next month or two. With a hopeful future in mind, I looked forward to what was to come.

Unfortunately, my hopefulness quickly faded after receiving an update in my portal just a week later. They either accepted me early or rejected me. Sadly, it was the latter. I was rejected from the BFA Musical Theatre program and redirected to the BA Theatre Studies program. However, this wasn't my dream. I was disappointed by how my senior year had, at the time, led to nothing. I struggled with how to move forward in my career, as there was nothing else I wanted to pursue, but I had to make a decision soon.

Looking for purpose as I wrapped up my senior year, our last project was to direct a scene from a play that was a part of our Theatre History curriculum. I was given the show "The Dumbwaiter," a comedy-drama written in 1960. I was very unsure how to approach this show, so I kept an open mind. During rehearsals with my cast, I experimented with the voice, circumstances, and the relationship between my two actors. The final project was this war-warped, Britain spoof that landed me an A+. Surprisingly, everyone in my class loved my scene, which was a new and unusual sensation for me. I wasn't the one performing, but the experience of helping actors and having my own vision brought to life was electrifying.

Motivated by this success, I looked back at Montclair State and the Theatre Studies program to see what they had to offer. In their program, it was a very well-rounded experience in everything theatre, with a Directing track in the making at the school. Performing is my entire life, but what would directing truly look like for me? My peers loved my scene, and it all came naturally to me, but could I still perform? The answer to all of these is the same: just because you walk through a door, doesn't mean it is closed.

I realize life won't always go as planned, and sometimes we must grieve who we were.

Reflecting on these changes, I realize life won't always go as planned, and sometimes we must grieve who we were. Moments happen for a reason, and if we hold onto them too long, letting go is hard. Sometimes, letting go and recognizing our progress is an accomplishment in itself. I miss performing, but I haven't given it up. I've found a new passion in directing. As a sophomore Directing student, I've worked with directors with varied international experience. I am currently an Assistant Director for a production, and I am preparing for a directing job this summer.

I still act and perform in different ways, just not as much as I used to, and that's okay. I am proud of the work that brought me here and the work ahead. I still grieve who I was before my new path, but I know change helps us become who we're meant to be.

Meet the Author - Theresa Fletcher

Theresa Fletcher is a mother of four, one of whom she carries in her heart. She is a proud grandmother of three and a devoted godmother of two. She has a devoted husband whose support has been a constant source of strength. Born and raised in Chester, Pennsylvania, she is deeply rooted in faith, family, and the power of resilience.

Theresa is a graduate of Chester High School and holds a Bachelor's degree in Human Services and a Master's degree in Healthcare Administration. With a heart for service, she worked at the Children's Hospital of Philadelphia and the University of Pennsylvania.

After experiencing the unimaginable loss of a child, Theresa found herself on a deeply personal journey through grief that changed her, challenged her, and inspired her to write. Through words, she offers an honest and compassionate look at the reality of grief and healing. Her hope is to reach others who are hurting, letting them know they are not alone, and reminding them that while life after loss is never the same, it is still possible to move forward.

Anchor Word: Growth

Paula's Prelude

Theresa writes with the wisdom of a mother who has lived through the unthinkable and still chooses gratitude. Her story isn't loud; it hums – steady, reflective, and true. She teaches us that growth doesn't mean moving on; it means learning to live with what love leaves behind. Through her souvenirs of memory and grace, she gives permission to every grieving parent to honor the ache while cherishing the gift of time shared.

Closure is not the end of the story
— it is the moment we choose
to honor what remains.
Every goodbye still holds grace.

Souvenirs of Love and Loss

Anchor Word: Growth

My journey offers comfort and recognition for those who feel alone. It proves that remembering is healing and that love never dies. The loss of a child is among the most devastating experiences a parent can face, shattering the heart beyond words. But sharing that loss opens a door for other grieving parents to enter a space of shared sorrow, resilience, love, and healing. Remembering our children—their smiles, laughter, and unique personalities—keeps them alive in our hearts and comforts us as we navigate the grief that comes with growing older. I still see his jaundiced, gold-colored eyes open as he shook his head no, showing he no longer wished to be here. I asked my sister, "Did you see him shake his head no?" She nodded as tears streamed down her face; it was a silent cry for both of us. In that moment, we both understood he was at peace with dying. We kept calling out names, hoping those he loved would give him a reason to live.

Saturday, June 10, 2023, at 10:46 am, my son passed away. My worst nightmare had come true. I remember everything so clearly, from stepping off the elevator and hearing the nurse say, "We have a code in progress, you have to wait," to her grabbing my hand and running me to his room. I was able to hold his still soft, warm hand; he softly squeezed mine, and then he took his last breath. Not all stories about loss end in despondency; some reveal a quiet path to healing and growth, a path I've walked since that day. My story is not a guide to "getting over" grief—there is no such thing. Instead, it offers a glimpse into my "new norm," as my world shifted with no return to life as it was. My son's death reshaped my life and sent my emotions on a roller coaster, a term I now use for the ups and downs I experience.

While the loss of my son was undeniably devastating, my life has gradually found a new sense of purpose and meaning. This meaning comes through building and honoring my son's memory. Trying to 'get over' such a catastrophic loss is impossible; instead, we learn to integrate it into our lives. We don't move on; we move forward, honoring our loved ones by keeping their memories and names alive. Even so, I often struggle to find ways to honor him and keep him present. At first, there were many posts and messages on his Facebook page—'I miss you,' 'I love you,' 'How do I go on without you?'—but now, such tributes appear less often. I wonder if people still remember him as much as before. This pattern reveals that life inevitably moves forward. More than ever, I realize people are not stuck; they have returned to their routines, and the world keeps spinning. They no longer call or ask; they just move on. I stay here, holding every memory and milestone close because it feels as if I must—if I don't, who will?

There is a lack of empathy for a person's grief. People are less invested until they are directly affected by losing a child. To cope with insensitivity, we must establish boundaries. We set them because empathy and understanding are often missing. We need our loved ones to acknowledge our pain, listen to us, and be present in our darkest moments. This empathy is essential for our well-being. People may not understand your world has shattered until they've lived it. Yet, some may still believe their world or grief is greater. No one's grief is more important; it cannot be measured or compared to anyone else's. Comparison only creates more boundaries, as grief varies from person to person. If you've grieved, you understand the feeling. So, do not suppress another's grief, because doing so is like diminishing their loss and their loved one.

I think a lot, I cry a lot; but more so than ever, I think about him more now than when he was alive. People say absence makes the heart grow fonder, but I wonder about the meaning of that when the absence of a child is permanent. Not a day goes by without thoughts of him. Grief is not a one-time event that we move past; it's a continuous process that becomes an integral part of us. I peel apart and reflect on every detail of his life, never wanting—even when the pain is great—to forget anything. Sometimes, even if I wanted to, I couldn't. I remember everything, from the day I wobbled into the hospital to have him to my last visit with him after his death. Stories circulate about loved ones visiting after they're gone —whether for comfort or as unmistakable signs—and I find myself questioning my own experiences. I've wondered if it was all a dream or something more, especially during one vivid moment that felt too real to dismiss: his question, "Mom, what does it mean when I take two steps and all I see is dirt?" My alarm went off before I could answer. Whether the experience was real or not, it left me feeling sad and crying silently that day. I never got to answer his question; I was brought back to reality too quickly. Boo-Boo, you're resting, you're at peace.

To this day, I still don't know if it was real, imagined, or grief. Grief is a complex, personal, and nuanced experience that is never the same for anyone. I used to say there's no book on being a perfect parent—and if there is, it's not true. Now, I say there is no perfect way to grieve—books can't teach it. Everyone experiences it differently; it can strike at any time, sometimes unexpectedly. Grief can make you cry all day, but the same thing that made you cry yesterday could bring a smile today.

During my most complex grieving moments, someone suggested I keep a journal. It was the best advice I ever received; it didn't seem helpful at first, but I see the difference now. Grief and pain are never eliminated; you learn to live with them because they never fully leave. You must grow with your grief and reshape yourself, as you can't reshape it. Dr. Paula Kea-Hollis once told me, "Grief comes in phases and stages." I understand that now. Grief is a process that requires time, care, and patience, much like caring for a newborn. Eventually, grief grows, changes, but still returns. I learned to be patient and open about my process. I learned to share when I was fragile or when my peace was disturbed. Peace became crucial for healing and growth. Once disrupted, I had to start reshaping myself again, riding that emotional roller coaster and trying to refocus on life.

You must grow with your grief and reshape yourself, as you can't reshape it.

That rollercoaster ride takes me up on some days and down on others. The lows are filled with "would have, could have, should have" thoughts—always wondering if I did enough. The fond memories of my son help during these moments. He was outgoing, funny, loved, and the life of the party. It wasn't until 2020 that his life changed. Something shifted, and he lost interest in himself and those around him. He pushed away the family that loved him deeply. We may never know why. I've learned to let go of questions and whispers about what happened—it was his story, and he chose not to share it.

My son turned to alcohol instead of telling me what was going on in his life. I know there is no coming back, but if I had one wish, it would be for him to tell me what made him want to leave. He didn't commit suicide, but he did not want to put the bottle down and stop drinking to prevent dying. Finding a coping mechanism to get through the day, to get through this thing called life. You hear people say, "How do you do it?", "If I lose a child, I will just die". You inhale; exhale; manage; cope; learn; and you live. You learn to live with the questions, you learn to live with the harmful comments, and you learn when and when not to respond. Not speaking in a bad way, but rather in a way that people often don't realize or understand how harmful words can be. If you have never lost a child, you will never understand the pain or unique emotion that parents feel from harmful yet unnecessary comments. Some people really don't know what to say. Unfortunately, I used to do the same thing. But after the loss of my son, I learned. I learned what to say, what not to say, and when not to say anything. Believe it or not, the presence of being there is more comforting than making conversation. A picture is like a thousand words; silence and a fond memory are golden.

I focus on memories; the ones I consider "souvenirs". Internal souvenirs that take me to a settled place about our love and what we shared. Some days it's like hopping from one happy memory to another. I smile, and I thank God for the moments that He allowed us to share. I thank Him for the thirty-five years that He let us have him. People thought I was crazy when I would say, It could have been worse. I could sit and wonder what my son would be like, what he would look like, what he would have been. God blessed me to see him grow into a young man, for him to live long enough to father his only child, grow gray hair, and shave his head to be bald. These are the best internal souvenirs that I was blessed to live long enough to see, remember, and cherish until the day I rest in peace. Memories can be powerful, but they can also be heartbreaking. It feels heartbreaking in a way that makes it seem as though time has stopped, yet it has passed so quickly. You carry an emotional weight that lingers for days, an emotional weight that can be described as an emotional hangover: nausea, headache, anxiety, stomach aches, and fatigue.

Experiencing a traumatic loss, such as the loss of a child, you reflect and ask, What did I do in my life that was so bad. I'm often told that God does not make mistakes and never to question God's work, but what else would one do when you bury your child? So, to not question God's work, I ask myself, "Was this my payback for my wrongdoings and in my young adult lifestyle? Did this come back to haunt my son? Did he pay for my sins? Was it because of me and the on-and-offs of going to church? Looking for meaning; is this how guilt, faith, and loss collide? This weight carried is not how grace is supposed to work, but I cannot shake the feeling that I may have opened the door for the pain that lives in me. There is an internal battle of trying to hold on to faith when you are not protected from an unimaginable loss. I have learned to express my anger, grief, pain, and, more importantly, I have learned how to give it to God. I have not received answers, but I accept His love and thank Him for the good things that I have.

Every day, I am increasingly accepting my new norm, this grieving journey that can be described as an emotional state of hopelessness and despair. Although I may not fully understand and disagree with his loss, I've acknowledged that this is my reality. This is the path and the hand I have been dealt; continuing to wake up every morning, remembering and carrying the love I have for him, with nowhere to go. I miss him and will probably never make sense of this whole thing called life, but I will move forward, I will continue to grow, inch by inch, day by day, carrying his memory, because my son is my souvenir, and so are the memories of him. If I could turn back the hands of time, knowing what I know now, I would never have had children. If I knew then that I would have a son only to have to bury him, I would never have had children. The pain of losing a child is so bad, so unbelievable, and so unbearable. I would not wish this on my worst enemy, and just as much, I pray not to lose another. The loss of a child is against the natural order, contrary to the natural course of life. Parents are not supposed to bury their children; children are supposed to bury their parents.

Selah

Closing Reflection

When I first imagined this anthology, I thought each story would fit neatly into one of the eight words in *The GIFT in Grief* framework – Gratitude, Growth, Introspection, Intentionality, Focus, Forward-thinking, Tenacity, and Transformation. But as these stories came to life, I realized that grief doesn't fit neatly into anything. It spills over lines, blurs edges, and reshapes the way we see ourselves and the world around us.

Not every word made its way into this first volume – and that, too, is a reflection of grief. Some lessons reveal themselves immediately; others take a lifetime. The words that remain unspoken are simply waiting for their season.

What has emerged in this book is a collective heartbeat – a tapestry of faith, love, and resilience that reminds us that grief is not an ending but an evolution. Each story is a sacred offering, proof that pain and purpose can coexist, that tears can water new growth, and that remembrance itself is an act of healing.

If these pages stirred something in you - a memory, a moment, or a message still unspoken - perhaps it is time to write your own. The next G.I.F.T. in Grief anthology is waiting for your story. To learn more, visit https://www.grief.paulahollis.com/anthology.

Turn the Page

The story of grief does not end; it continues to reveal new chapters of grace, growth, and healing.

If the stories within this book met you in your grief, then the next step is to meet yourself in grace.

📖 **Explore the companion devotional:**
Graced to Grieve: A 40-day journey to unwrap the G.I.F.T. in Grief
Scan the QR code below or visit Amazon.com https://a.co/d/ayE85tN to begin your 40-day journey of reflection and renewal.

"Grace doesn't erase grief; it helps you read your story differently."
— *Paula Hollis*

About the Author

Dr. Paula Kea Hollis is a life transitions coach, author, and founder of *House of Growth*™. Known for her reflective frameworks and acronym-driven teachings, she guides others through healing, purpose, and transformation with grace and grounded wisdom. Through her ministry, writing, and coaching, Paula helps individuals discover that grief is not something to fix — it's something to flow through. She lives her message daily, honoring her late husband Martin's legacy while helping others grow through theirs.

Learn more about her grief work at:
www.grief.paulahollis.com

Learn more about her other offerings at:
www.coachlinks.paulahollis.com

Email: coachpaula@paulahollis.com

All Social Media: @iampaulahollis

Made in the USA
Coppell, TX
04 January 2026

68065532R00114